A PRACTICAL GUIDE TO THE
THEMATIC APPERCEPTION TEST

A PRACTICAL GUIDE TO THE THEMATIC APPERCEPTION TEST

The TAT in Clinical Practice

Edward Aronow, Ph.D.
Montclair State University

Kim Altman Weiss, Ph.D.
New York Presbyterian Hospital

Marvin Reznikoff, Ph.D.
Fordham University

USA	Publishing Office:	BRUNNER-ROUTLEDGE *A member of the Taylor & Francis Group* 325 Chestnut Street Philadelphia, PA 19106 Tel: (215) 625 8900 Fax: (215) 625-2940
	Distribution Center:	BRUNNER-ROUTLEDGE *A member of the Taylor & Francis Group* 7625 Empire Drive Florence, KY 41042 Tel: 1-800-634-7064 Fax: 1-800-248-4724
UK		BRUNNER-ROUTLEDGE *A member of the Taylor & Francis Group* 27 Church Road Hove E. Sussex, BN3 2FA Tel: +44 (0) 1273 207411 Fax: +44 (0) 1273 205612

A PRACTICAL GUIDE TO THE THEMATIC APPERCEPTION TEST: The TAT in Clinical Practice

3 4 5 6 7 8 9 0

Printed by Sheridan Books, Ann Arbor, MI.
Cover design by Nancy Abbott.

A CIP catalog record for this book is available from the British Library.

⊚ The paper in this publication meets the requirements of the ANSI Standard Z39.48-1984 (Permanence of Paper).

Library of Congress Cataloging-in-Publication Data

Aronow, Edward.
      A practical guide to the thematic apperception test : the T.A.T. in clinical practice / Edward Aronow, Kim Altman Weiss, Marvin Reznikoff.
      p. cm.
Includes index.
ISBN 0-87630-944-9 (alk. paper)
      1. Thematic Apperception Test. I. Weiss, Kim Altman. II. Reznikoff, Marvin. III. Title.

BF698.8.T5 A7 2001
155.2'844—dc21   2001027392

ISBN 0-87630-944-9

To Drs. Lon Gieser and Wes Morgan—
two dedicated TAT historians.

To Christiana Morgan—an early TAT pioneer.

CONTENTS

INTRODUCTION

The purpose of the present text, as its name implies, is to provide the student with a short, manageable, but also reasonably comprehensive guide to the Thematic Apperception Test (TAT) and other apperceptive techniques.

As the present authors have stated elsewhere (Aronow, Reznikoff, & Moreland, 1994), the TAT, like the Rorschach, provides essentially *idiographic* rather than *nomothetic* information. Thus, it is quite effective in telling the clinician how the subject views the self and the world in his or her own unique way. It is less effective as a psychometric procedure, providing a nomothetic measure of traits. For this reason, we prefer the term *technique* when dealing with projective devices, reserving the term *test* for those instruments that are primarily nomothetic (e.g., Millon Adolescent Personality Inventory-2, MMPI-2). Rossini and Moretti (1997) have correspondingly remarked on the resulting tendency of TAT applications in clinical practice to abandon both any psychometric approach or scoring system.

The present text will cover both the well-known TAT and the Children's Apperception Test (CAT), and will also foray into the somewhat lesser known cousins of these techniques that have come into the testing arena in recent years. Subject populations that will be considered include children, adolescents, and adults. Some scoring systems that have been put forward will be discussed but, as we will state, we do not view scoring systems for apperceptive techniques as time-effective. Their usefulness is, thus, principally limited to research on apperceptive techniques. This book will also give special attention to cross-cultural issues and the application of apperceptive techniques to minority populations.

The text is organized as follows: Chapter 1 will discuss the history of apperception techniques, with Chapter 2 devoted to test administration.

The third chapter will present test interpretation, including the use of the one-sentence summary technique that we find very helpful. Scoring systems will be briefly presented in the context of this chapter.

Chapter 4 will present data on the stimulus value of the TAT cards. The fifth chapter will succinctly describe research findings pertaining to apperceptive techniques, while Chapter 6 will deal with diversity issues and alternative apperceptive methods. The seventh chapter will cover the TAT and psychotherapy, while Chapter 8 will describe how apperceptive findings should be integrated in a psychological report. The final chapter, Chapter 9, will present sample protocols.

A History of Apperception Techniques

The prehistory of projective techniques goes back quite far, including works of the ancient Greeks on stimulus ambiguity, comments by Da Vinci on the artistic usefulness of discerning objects in the mud or the embers of a fire, and Shakespeare's comments on "cloud interpretation."

For instance, in the 15th century, Leonardo Da Vinci quoted Botticelli as stating that when a sponge full of various colors is thrown against a wall, a blot is produced in which figures of people, various animals, and so on, may be perceived. Da Vinci suggested the use of perceptions such as these for artistic inspiration (cited in Zubin, Eron, & Schumer, 1965). He stated:

> Don't take my advice lightly when I advise you, even though it may appear boring to stop and gaze at wall spots, or at the ashes in the fire, in the clouds, or in the mud and at similar things; you will, if you consider it carefully, discover in it many wonderful things. For the painter's spirit is aroused to new things by it, be it in composition of battles, of animals and men, or in the various compositions of landscapes and of unusual things such as devils, and their like, which are calculated to bring you honor. Through the indescribable and indefinite things, the spirit becomes awakened to new discoveries. (Da Vinci, quoted in Zubin et al., 1965, p. 167)

Binet and Henri, the founders of modern intelligence testing, are usually given credit as the originators of the scientific approach to projective techniques, using inkblots in the study of visual imagination (Binet & Henri, 1896). Binet and Henri also used children's reactions to pictures as measures of intellect.

The TAT was first developed by Murray and his coworkers at the Harvard Psychological Clinic, having first been described by Morgan and Murray (1935). The term *apperception* was chosen in view of the fact that subjects don't just perceive, rather, they construct stories about the cards in accordance with their personality characteristics and their experiences (Anderson, 1999). As contrasted with the Rorschach, the TAT has usually been regarded as providing more structure to the subject. As Murray noted in the test manual, the original procedure required two one-hour sessions with 10 cards used in each session. Those cards used in the second session were chosen to be more unusual, with subjects asked to give free play to their imaginations.

There has been controversy about the early history of the TAT in that Christiana Morgan was, at the initial stages, given the first authorship on the TAT. The controversy was magnified because of the long, conflictual relationship between Morgan and Murray. Douglas (1993) has suggested that the downgrading of Christiana Morgan in the authorship of the TAT is an example of male chauvinism, though most current authors view Murray as the primary force behind the TAT (e.g., Morgan, 1995). There is general agreement that the idea for the TAT emerged from an in-class question asked by one of Murray's undergraduate students. The student reported that her son, when ill, had spent the day making up stories about pictures in magazines. This mother wondered if pictures might be used in a clinical setting to release fantasy material (Douglas, 1993).

The TAT quickly became one of the most popular and sometimes *the* most popular projective technique in the clinician's armamentarium. Obrzut and Boliek (1986) describe thematic picture techniques as "the most widespread projective techniques used with children and adolescents" (p. 176). Similarly, Piotrowski and Keller (1984) found that clinical program directors most often cited the TAT as the projective test with which trained psychologists should be familiar. Lubin, Larsen, and Matarazzo (1984) and Watkins, Cambell, Nieberding, and Hallmark (1995) have likewise reported the instrument's continuing popularity among projective techniques in a variety of situations and populations. The TAT and similar thematic instruments have been found to be frequently used for assessment in cross-cultural research (Retief, 1987). A good grounding in the interpretation of apperception techniques thus appears highly desirable.

The TAT appears to have received better acceptance in the scientific community than, for example, the Rorschach. It should also be noted that the

TAT is known for its nonclinical contributions as well, being an important technique used in various areas of personality research; as for example, McClelland's works on the *need for achievement* (e.g., McClelland, 1958, 1961a, 1961b). These more strictly scientific applications of the TAT have probably facilitated its acceptance by research-oriented psychologists.

A number of other projective story techniques have been put forward subsequent to the TAT. These have included the CAT designed by Bellak (Bellak & Abrams, 1997); the CAT-H, using human figures for older children (Bellak & Hurvich, 1966); the Roberts Apperception Test for Children (RATC; McArthur & Roberts, 1982); the Blacky Pictures Test (Blum, 1950); the Make-A-Picture Story Test (MAPS; Shneidman, 1952); the School Apperception Method (SAM; Soloman & Starr, 1968); the Michigan Pictures Test Revised (MPTR; Hutt, 1980); the Gerontological Apperception Test (GAT; Wolk & Wolk, 1971); the Senior Apperception Technique (SAT; Bellak & Abrams); the Tell-Me-A-Story (TEMAS; Constantino, Malgady & Vazquez, 1981); and the Southern Mississippi TAT (SM-TAT; Ritzler, Sharkey, & Chudy, 1980).

In addition, the TAT itself has been adapted at times for certain special purposes by modifying the original set of pictures, such as in attitude surveys evaluating the attitudes toward issues such as labor problems and authority (e.g., Harrison, 1965). Another type of TAT modification involves the intensive measurement of a single characteristic such as sex or aggression. The studies by McClelland and his associates (mentioned earlier) on need for achievement (nAch), utilizing two of the TAT cards along with two other pictures, represent an especially impressive body of research.

Series D of the TAT has been in use for many years; previous Series A, B, and C were designed to be used by gluing pictures onto a cardboard background. Murstein (1963) has described the selection of cards for Series D, with cards being chosen on the basis of their contribution to establishing diagnoses for various clients.

Many people associated with the Harvard Psychological Clinic are reported to have contributed pictures, with artistic work being done by Christiana Morgan and Samuel Thal (Morgan, 1995). Morgan has also noted that the modifications of original images and earlier TAT representations were generally in the direction of removing detail and complexity and increasing ambiguity—thereby presumably increasing the likelihood of projection.

From its inception, the TAT has steadfastly remained a widely used test in clinical settings. It has spawned many variations having research and clinical applications. From the standpoint of both its historical antecedents and current usage, it is very likely that it will continue to be an important instrument in the area of personality assessment.

2

CHAPTER

Test Administration

When to Use the TAT

The TAT is not unique, in that information obtained may overlap with information received from an interview, observation, and other projective techniques. However, the TAT does draw attention to and elicit specific types of material more than other methods, particularly interpersonal aspects of psychodynamics. Responses are content-rich, and reveal the subject's outlook in relationships with authority figures, subordinates, and same and opposite sex peers. This material can be useful, for example, in determining the match between a subject and a specific type of psychotherapy, and can be used to enhance the psychotherapeutic process. The TAT should generally be considered only one of the tests in a standard test battery.

Materials

The advantages of the TAT include the relative simplicity of administration and the ease with which the materials are able to be transported. The examiner needs a set of TAT cards, an 8½" x 11" pad of paper, a writing instrument to record responses, and possibly an audio recorder (if desired). A clipboard may be useful to the examiner for holding and discreetly recording responses.

☐ Setting

The TAT, as well as other tests in the battery, should be administered in a well-lit, comfortable, quiet room that will allow the subject to be free from interruptions and distractions. The subject should be seated in a chair at an edge of the table or desk adjacent to the examiner. This arrangement allows the examiner to look at the cards from the perspective of the subject, and prevents the table or desk from being a barrier between the examiner and the examinee.

☐ Rapport

Before beginning any test administration procedures, it is suggested that the examiner ask the subject if he or she knows the purpose of the testing, in order to better understand the meaning the test procedure has for the individual. The examiner should clear up misconceptions regarding how the test results will be used and any confidentiality issues relevant to the situation, and endeavor to establish proper rapport through presenting a reasonably friendly attitude. The examiner could possibly begin by talking briefly about some non-threatening topics.

☐ Which Cards to Give

There are 31 cards in the entire set, and Murray intended that subjects be administered 20. It seems that this number of cards is sufficient to lend a representative sample of the subjects' "fantasy" (Zubin et al., 1965). Some of the cards were meant to be used for all subjects, and some are supposedly only appropriate according to the sex and age of the subject and are so designated on the back of the card. However, because of time constraints and the fact that the TAT is often administered as part of a battery, 10–14 cards are more typically given. The present authors suggest even fewer in the interests of practicality.

Some researchers and clinicians ordinarily use the male set of TAT cards with men, and the female set of TAT cards with women, because it is believed that on the TAT examinees identify more with stimulus characters of the same sex as themselves, and therefore produce more projective material when the stimulus figures match their own sex. Katz, Russ, and Overholser (1993) conducted a study to test this assumption, however, and their results do not support it. A significant effect of gender was not found for amount of fantasy, amount of affect, intensity of affect, or length of story for any of the cards administered. This study does not recommend the use of separate sets of TAT cards for men and women.

Clinicians often choose to administer cards that are related to their hypotheses about the subject's problems. However, it is inadvisable to administer only cards that the examiner believes will have particular "pull" for the individual subject, based on suspected areas of conflict (Rosenwald, 1968). This practice results in an unrepresentative or biased view of the subject. Rapaport, Gill, and Schafer (1968) suggest that the cards that do not have as much personal meaning for the subject may provide a baseline performance for evaluating the more personally relevant cards.

Hartman (1970) asked 90 psychologists to rank their choice of cards, which resulted in the following recommendation for a standard set of eight TAT cards: 1, 2, 3BM, 4, 6BM, 7BM, 8BM, and 13MF. This set has been criticized (Bellak & Abrams, 1997) because all of these cards are meant for men, and none are meant particularly for women. Bellak suggested substituting card 7GF for card 7BM, and adding cards 9GF and 10 to create a more balanced basic set. In our experience card 12F may be far more useful and provocative than card 10, the latter often eliciting stereotyped, unrevealing themes. Other cards may be added if the examiner believes that they may yield fruitful material specific to the subject's conflicts.

The cards are usually administered in numerical order. However, a study by Terry (1952) indicated that the order of administration does not have an impact on the emotional tone, outcome, or level of response of the stories.

Although it is not one of the more commonly used cards (Hartman, 1970), Kahn (1984) suggested that the blank card, # 16, is a very useful card to use because it is completely neutral, simple, and culture-free. Other cards have been criticized as being overly negative, too complex for children, or oriented toward the middle class. The blank card is not amenable to such criticism, and on the contrary, is the ideal unstructured projective stimulus. Because of the absolute lack of external stimulus, one can be assured that the response is based completely on internal factors, and therefore is likely to be meaningful.

Problems with the use of the blank card can be attributed largely to poor instructions for its use. Kahn (1984) suggested the following instructions as the blank card is given to the subject: "This card is different from the others. This time you get to make up the picture, too. Tell me a complete story based on *your* picture just like in the other cards, and tell me what is happening, what led up to it, and what will happen in the end." These clear and simple instructions emphasize the similarity between the blank card and the other cards, and remind the subject to produce a story rather than a descriptive scene. It is recommended that the blank card be administered last, which highlights the special nature of the task. "White responses," such as "a polar bear in the snow," are considered rejections of the card, and may reflect hostility toward the examiner and the procedure.

☐ Instructions

Murray's (1943) suggestions for instructing a subject are the following:

> This is a test of imagination, one form of intelligence. I am going to show you some pictures, one at a time; and your task will be to make up as dramatic a story as you can for each. Tell what has led up to the event shown in the picture, describe what is happening at the moment, what the characters are feeling and thinking, and then give the outcome. Speak your thoughts as they come to your mind. Do you understand? Since you have 50 minutes for 10 pictures, you can devote about five minutes to each story. Here is the first picture. (p. 46)

The above instructions are simplified slightly for children and adults of limited education.

We suggest that the examiner eliminate, "This is a test of imagination, one form of intelligence," and "Your task will be to make up as dramatic a story as you can." The five-minute time limit instruction can also be removed. It is felt that these are unnecessary and may be distracting. If the subject talks too long, then it would be acceptable for the examiner to ask him or her to finish up and go on to the next card.

The instructions should be repeated on request. Parts of the instructions may have to be repeated later on, such as reminding the subject to tell you the characters' thoughts and feelings, or to create an ending for the story. After repeating a specific instruction on several cards, the examiner may choose to cease to remind the subject of missing parts of the story. However, it should be noted which parts of the instructions must be repeated persistently, as this gives information regarding what is difficult for the subject and can be quite meaningful.

It may be helpful to put the four questions on a card in front of subjects (possibly on an index card) in order to remind them of the components to include without interrupting their flow. With slight modification of instructions, the TAT can be self-administered or group administered.

The cards are kept facedown in front of the examiner, with the first card to be administered on top. The examiner presents the cards to the subject one at a time. Cards are placed face-down by the subject as they are completed.

☐ Recording the Responses

Record the stories and any other utterances verbatim, including pauses, questions, off-the-record remarks, and additional verbalizations that may not be meant to be part of the story. If the subject speaks too quickly, then it is acceptable to ask him or her to speak more slowly so that you are able to record the stories word for word.

Rosenwald (1968) suggested that the responses be recorded by hand, and as part of the instructions the subject should be told to speak slowly so that the examiner is able to write it all down. Rosenwald asserts that the subject's compliance with this request will yield useful information about his or her empathy and self-restraint. This information would be lost by the use of a recording device, or by allowing the subject to write down his or her own stories.

Asking the subject to speak slowly so that you can record verbatim is preferable to asking the subject to repeat his or her story when you fall behind, because it is common that the subject will alter stories on repetition (Rapaport et al., 1968). If a subject asks what you are writing down, or if you are writing all their remarks, respond truthfully that you are recording the stories and other remarks as they say them as part of the standardized administration procedure.

Baty and Dreger (1975) conducted a study to compare three common methods of recording TAT protocols: machine recording, subjects recording their own stories, and the examiner recording the stories. The stories yielded were contrasted in the degree to which they revealed personality. Seventy-two undergraduate subjects were administered the TAT on three occasions, each time utilizing a different recording method. While there were no significant differences in mean number of content categories using the three methods, it appeared that a great deal of material was lost when the examiner recorded the stories by hand. It was concluded that recording by machine and by the subject are the most efficient methods. Machine recording, of course, requires lengthy transcription and may miss accompanying behavior. A subject may, on the other hand, resist self-recording because of alleged poor spelling and writing skills.

When the examiner is recording, abbreviations are useful in cutting down writing time. Commonly used abbreviations the examiner may find helpful include:

ll	=	looks like	bec	=	because
dk	=	don't know	et	=	everything
cd	=	could	wd	=	would
w	=	with	r	=	are
st	=	something	c	=	see
so	=	someone	u	=	you

Behavioral observations should be recorded. Body language, facial expressions, posture, hand movements, tone of voice, pauses, attention, and motivation all provide information useful to interpretation of the stories.

During TAT administration, subjects will often ask the examiner questions to reduce the ambiguity of the situation. The examiner should take care that his or her answers do not lead the subject and ruin the intended ambiguity important to the purpose of the test. When asked for guidance in creating responses, the examiner should answer ambiguously, using statements such as "as you wish," "as you think best," and "there are no right or wrong answers." Overall, it is best for the examiner to say nothing throughout the testing unless absolutely necessary, in order to avoid leading the subject.

If a subject's verbalizations are simply descriptive of the picture, remind the subject of the questions to be answered by the story: what is happening, characters' thoughts and feelings, what led up to it, how it all turns out. It may also help to remind the subject that he or she is to make up a story that moves beyond the picture per se. Descriptions may be viewed as refusals (Rapaport et al., 1968). The subject might be gently reminded that the examiner is interested in a story plot, not just a description of the picture.

If the subject goes on too long by becoming overly detailed, the examiner may ask the subject to make up an ending for the story, and suggest that they go on to the next one. The examiner may tell the subject that the stories need not be so long.

If a subject tells only short constricted stories, the examiner might ask him or her to tell a longer story, or to "let go" more (Bellak & Abrams, 1997, p. 58). A hesitant subject might be prompted by saying "So?," "Well?,"

"What comes to mind?," or "What are you thinking?"

If the subject gives many "or" responses, and vacillates between possible choices, the examiner may ask the subject, "Which is it?" and have the subject choose.

☐ Inquiry

An inquiry stage may be used as an adjunct to the subject's free responses where there are ambiguities or idiosyncratic elements. At this time, the examiner can clarify responses, and obtain more information. Bellak and Abrams (1997) suggested that the examiner ask for associations to names, dates, places, or any other specific material given by the subject. It is felt, however, that information obtained in an inquiry is not as interpretively useful as spontaneously offered material (Rosenwald, 1968).

Rapaport et al. (1968) outlined types of inquiries that can be made. Firstly, inquiries can be made when there is lack of clarity on a number of levels. Secondly, inquiry into perceptual unclarity is important to the discovery of pathology and possibly psychoses. Perceptual unclarities include distorting the present stimuli or overlooking prominent stimuli. Inquiry can help distinguish slips of the tongue from greater perceptual misrecognition indicative of different pathology. Inquiry into verbal unclarity involves asking the subject about slips of the tongue, in order to find out if the subject meant what was said. This can be done by immediately interrupting the story, under the guise of trying to accurately follow or record, and simply repeating the phrase in question and seeing if the subject corrects or repeats it. Inquiries into meanings of the story that are unclear should also be made. Repeating the instructions and asking the subject for parts of the story omitted—such as what led up to the picture, and what the characters are thinking—can also be considered part of the inquiry phase. The examiner should try to get the subject to make decisions and be specific about his or her responses.

Some examiners (e.g., Bellak & Abrams, 1997) believe that the inquiry should be done after all the stories are completed so that the inquiry does not impact on subsequent stories. However, Rosenwald (1968) suggested inquiries immediately following each story, while the story is still fresh in the subject's mind. Inquiries about gaps, vagueness, and mix-ups in the narrative should be clarified.

We recommend that inquiries should be the exception rather than the rule, and, if done, should be done immediately following each story. This procedure guards against the subject being overwhelmed by questions at the completion of the TAT, and reduces the likelihood of the examiner being viewed as a "grand inquisitor." All inquiries should be nonsuggestive and nonleading. "The more noncommittal the inquiry, the more significant the answer" (Rapaport et al., 1968, p. 477).

☐ Testing Children

When administering the TAT to a child, there are some special considerations to keep in mind. The examiner should be more concerned with establishing sufficient rapport with a child than with an older individual, because children may be slower to warm up to a stranger. Becoming overly authoritarian is also to be especially avoided with children. The examiner should take great care to gear his or her language to the cognitive level of the child, in order to enhance rapport and to help the child understand the instructions for the task at hand. The examiner should be sensitive to the fact that children have a lower attention span than many adults, and may need a break in the middle of administration.

On the other hand, the same instructions may be used with children and adults. If an inquiry is used, immediate rather than delayed inquiry is recommended with children. We suggest that the TAT should not be administered to subjects under the age of 5 (though a very mature 4-year-old might still be a test subject).

☐ Impact of Race on the Examiner

There has been concern in contemporary testing that the race or the racial match of the examinee and examiner has an effect on test results. Although this issue has not been thoroughly investigated, we have found no compelling evidence to support this concern.

One study found that race of subject, race of examiner, racial match between subject and examiner, and race of stimulus figures do not have an impact on assessment of need for achievement and power using the TAT (Lefkowitz & Fraser, 1980). This study failed to support the common assumption that racially congruent stimuli or examiners increase identification, and thus impact TAT responses, influencing productivity.

Interpretation

☐ Theory

TAT responses can be meaningfully interpreted because it is assumed that what an individual makes of an ambiguous stimulus, such as TAT cards, reflects his or her own personality and characteristic modes of interacting with the environment. Subjects create TAT stories based on a combination of three things: the card stimulus, the testing environment, and the personality or inner world of the subject (Murstein, 1959). On the TAT, the degree of ambiguity of the stimulus varies from card to card, but each requires the individual to subjectively interpret the pictures and create a story, which involves borrowing on events from one's own experiences, feelings, and conflicts (Worchel & Dupree, 1990). Interpreting information obtained from a testing situation is ordinarily a useful way to obtain access to an individual's psychological makeup because when the subject is reacting to pictures, rather than real people and real social situations, he or she is under less pressure from conventionality and is more likely to depict his or her inner feelings (Reznikoff & Dollin, 1961). In addition to the actual TAT stories, the subject's behavior during testing also provides useful data, as behavior during psychological assessment can be seen as a sample of more generalized behavior. Interpretation involves discerning common factors underlying the various stories (both their content and form) and behavior observed during testing, and translating these themes into meaningful explanations of the subject's personality.

☐ Scoring Systems

Several scoring systems have been developed in order to help standardize interpretation of TAT material. Murray's (1943) original scoring system involved analyzing every sentence of every story, taking note of and ranking the needs (motives and feelings) of the main character and *press* (opposing forces in the environment). Interactions between need and press and outcomes were also taken into account. Partly due to the somewhat unwieldy, time-consuming nature of Murray's method, this system has not been widely used by psychologists.

Many other scoring systems have been developed to measure single or multiple variables such as aggression (Davids & Rosenblatt, 1958; Hafner & Kaplan, 1960), achievement (McClelland, Atkinson, Clark, & Lowell, 1953), object relations (Westen, 1991; Westen et al., 1991), and depression (Aaron, 1967); and some have attempted to be more comprehensive (Tompkins, 1947; Zubin et al., 1965).

In an ambitious attempt to create a relatively objective, inclusive scoring system, Zubin et al. (1965) presented scales for each particular card and general scales to rate stories for emotional tone and outcome. Separate norms by age, sex, education, and so on are provided, as well as the percentage of subjects who have any given number or more of stories of each degree of emotional tone. The authors report good interrater reliability. However, like Murray's system, Zubin et al.'s seems too cumbersome to use for interpretation of every card, and still only addresses limited aspects of the stories. Perhaps more practical than the aforementioned scoring system, Zubin et al. also presented frequency counts that estimate the frequency of occurrence of various features of stories not accounted for in the rating scales. The frequency counts cover themes, perceptual distortions, identity of character and objects, and deviations from instructions. The checklist provided is quite detailed. The advantages of frequency counts or checklists are that they can be used to highlight abstruse aspects of TAT responses that need to be pursued in a more comprehensive interpretive fashion (Zubin et al., 1965).

It appears that there exists a trade-off between comprehensiveness and practicality in scoring systems. Perhaps none has achieved widespread acceptance or usage (Dana, 1985) because each basically addresses only limited areas of personality, or takes too much time to use. When scoring systems are employed, information not addressed by that system is essentially lost. This is regrettable, as variables of interest in personality are infinite. Scoring systems are more appropriate for research purposes than clinical purposes unless one is interested in specific, predetermined areas or variables (Karon, 1981). Karon asserts that "the human mind is the only computer which can consider alternative hypotheses in sufficient complexity and diversity to winnow through the information involved in the TAT" (p. 97). Although exclusive use of scoring systems is not recommended, we suggest that examiners read through various scoring systems to get a feel for the types and the complexity of the variables they might want to include in interpretation, as well as becoming roughly familiar with norms.

☐ Main Themes Technique

Bellak and Abrams (1997) introduced an analysis sheet to be completed for each story. It summarizes information regarding the hero (main character), the hero's needs and drives, view of the world and people, conflicts, anxieties, defenses, and integration of the ego. In addition, these authors suggested that the examiner write brief summaries of the themes presented in the TAT stories, and write these summaries on three levels, ranging from relatively concrete to more abstract. The descriptive theme is the one nearest to observation, with the interpretive and diagnostic becoming increasingly observation-distant. The descriptive theme briefly restates the story in the third person, using simple words. The interpretive theme is a more generalized restatement of the story, using "one" as the subject. This assumes a meaning beyond the story. The diagnostic version interprets the previous themes using knowledge of psychodynamics, including stating conflicts, defenses, and interpersonal patterns. Impressions are turned into definitive statements.

The following is an example based on the story of a 24-year-old female:

> *Card 4:* Someone pissed this guy off and he's gonna defend his manlihood and return the blow or get into a fight and she doesn't want him to go. She's begging him—she cares—I think that she calms him and talks sense into him and his rage mellows out and he doesn't go off to fight.

Descriptive theme: A rageful man is stopped from fighting with someone who angered him by an imploring, concerned woman who reasons with him and calms him down.

Interpretive theme: When one's masculinity is threatened, one seeks revenge, but a female figure intervenes and successfully prevents aggressive retaliation.

Diagnostic theme: Reacts with anger to threatened masculinity, but conflicted over expressing aggressive drives. The anger is repressed. Females seen as concerned, comforting, and persuasively rational.

Writing summaries on these three levels is meant to ground the examiner and reduce the chance of "wild interpretations" by proceeding with interpretation in a step-by-step manner, from observation-near to observation-distant.

The present authors find that summarizing the TAT themes is very useful. Summaries may be called *main themes* that are simply short, descriptive restatements of the essence of the stories. Main themes should be written out for each story. More than one theme may be present in any given TAT story. Main themes are helpful in that glancing over the brief statements during interpretation renders the commonalties and repetitions in themes across stories more salient to the examiner.

☐ Nomothetic and Idiographic Interpretation

A combination of both nomothetic and idiographic methods yields the most comprehensive and valid TAT interpretations. *Nomothetic* refers to comparing the subject's responses to a normative comparison sample, in order to determine the degree of unusualness of the responses. This helps guard against interpreting responses as pathological that may be quite common and, alternatively, failing to recognize responses that are rare, and therefore particularly meaningful. This also aids in understanding to what degree the subject sees the world in a conventional manner (reality testing), and determining the extent to which the subject is defending against self-disclosure by limiting creative or unusual responses. In general, comparison to normative data aids the examiner in isolating personalized aspects of the protocol that are likely to be especially revealing, as well as pointing to cards that have particular meaning for subjects. Norms help ensure that relevant elements are noticed (Zubin et al., 1965). Eron (1950) presents norms for emotional tone and outcome based on 20 TAT cards for adult males and subsequently for adult females (Eron, 1953). Norms for themes are also noted according to a checklist of more than 100 themes. These norms are quite detailed. However, using nomothetic data alone leaves the risk of losing all meaningful data about areas not addressed in the norms. Another limitation is that relying on nomothetic data may encourage an overemphasis on discrete elements rather than an integrated personality picture, and one may "lose the forest for the trees."

The *idiographic* approach involves examining the individual subject's record and discerning meaning from the particular responses he or she chose. During this kind of analysis, the examiner asks him- or herself, "Why would a human being say that, out of all the possibilities that exist?" (Karon, 1981). Understanding the personalized story is the crux of interpretation. This type of method allows the examiner to maximally personalize the written report, doing justice to the individuality of responses. However, without the grounding provided by good norms, some interpretations may be off-track.

Both nomothetic and idiographic methods should be used in TAT interpretation. The degree of unusualness of the response as well as the idiosyncratic meaning to the subject are both important pieces contributing to a thorough interpretation. Comparison to norms is useful in putting the response in broader perspective, particularly for the beginning examiner. However, even when the general plot may be common, the details are often distinctive, perhaps by the choice of verbs and adjectives, or by use of proper names and dates (Rosenwald, 1968). Common themes can be used in idiographic ways. The complexity and individuality of idiographic interpretation, along with regular comparison to normative data, yields the most comprehensive and valid TAT interpretations.

☐ Areas of Interpretation

The examiner must be aware of what to look for as he or she reads TAT stories in order to recognize personally revealing material that will be useful in interpretation. The following section is provided to that end. The most common potential domains for analysis are discussed, although it would be impossible to include every possible source of fruitful information. It also should be emphasized that each of the following areas of interpretation should not be addressed in every testing protocol, as the resulting report would be too long, and the most important interpretations would be diluted by material less relevant for the individual subject in terms of the reasons the subject was referred for testing. All of the following areas should, however, be at least *considered* during interpretation.

The following are suggestions as to where examiners should focus their attention as they are considering responses to TAT assessment. The areas of interpretation are broken into three categories: story content, story structure, and behavior observations.

Story Content

Examiners should interpret the actual content of the stories subjects tell in response to the TAT cards. The most fruitful material for interpretation usually comes from focusing attention on the hero or main character of the stories, the relationships between characters in the stories, the manner in which the environment is depicted, and the outcomes of the stories.

The Hero

The examiner can discern much information about the subject by examining the hero of the story. The hero can be identified by looking for the character most spoken of, the one whose feelings and subjective notions are most discussed, the one who initiates important activities, or the figure with whom the subject seems to identify. If it is unclear, the hero is usually the figure most resembling the subject in age, sex, or other characteristics (Bellak & Abrams, 1997).

The needs and drives of the hero are likely to be related to the subject's needs and drives. For example, a hero who is ambitious and works persistently may indicate the subject's need for achievement. A hero who seeks the company of others may reveal the subject's need for affiliation; one who destroys property or hurts people demonstrates a strong aggressive drive. The direction of aggressive drives (out or in) is a useful piece of information. For example, a hero who smashes a sculpture would be assumed to direct his or her aggression outward, whereas one who speeds his or her car into a tree would be assumed to have inner-directed aggression.

The behaviors of the hero are usually a mixture of behavioral needs and wishes or fantasies of the subject. It is important but sometimes quite difficult to try to distinguish between latent needs and overt behavior. The psychologist may use biographical or background information and behavioral observations to help distinguish between them. The examiner can also look to characteristics of the hero to discern how acceptable the subject's needs and drives are to the self. More objectionable characteristics are also ordinarily attributed to characters far away in age, sex, or place from the subject, as an attempt at distancing (Dana, 1985). Indicators of distance should be noted and related to particular cards. Sometimes there is a second hero in the story, who often presents drives and sentiments more objectionable to the subject. Aspects of the subject's overt behavior may be revealed when the opposite occurs; that is, when the subject loses distance and tells patently biographical stories.

The subject's ego functioning (which includes the subject's self-perception, sense of competence, judgment, and personality integration) is revealed in the subject's depiction of the hero. The examiner should examine the subject's attitudes toward the hero, as this often reflects his or her own self-view. Additionally, the hero's ability to reach his or her goals illustrates the subject's sense of competence. To evaluate the quality of the subject's judgment, one may look to the adequacy of the hero's decisions and evaluations of the consequences of his or her actions.

Additional information about the subject's ego-functioning is obtained by evaluating the extent to which conflicting demands of the superego, id, and outside world are integrated. In particular, the adequacy of the subject's superego can be seen by evaluating if the hero's "punishments" are appropriate for experienced "crimes." Are the punishments overly harsh or lenient? If punishments seems to be inconsistent, perhaps the superego is not well integrated. The adequacy of the balance between the id and ego may be analyzed by examining the hero's ability to delay gratification and express drives and feelings in neither an overcontrolled nor undercontrolled way.

The subject's conflicts are exemplified by those of the hero. It should be noted which drives are in conflict with the hero's superego or the environment, and which drives are in conflict with each other. Similar to conflicts, the subject's anxieties are revealed in the hero's fears and discomforts.

The hero's reactions to such conflicts and anxieties reveal the subject's defensive structure. Briefly, defenses are intrapsychic processes that block distressing material (impulses, conflicts) from an individual's awareness (for a detailed explanation of defenses and their interpretation, see Schafer, 1954). The examiner should take note of how adequate the reactions, or defenses, are in warding off anxiety or depression by examining story material and the subject's behavior subsequent to the defensive expression. This will give an indication of how adaptive the employed defenses are, or if they interfere with adaptive functioning. One can also consult *The Diagnostic and Statistical Manual of Mental Disorders* (DSM-IV, 4th ed; American Psychiatric Association, 1994), which provides a Defensive Functioning Scale indicating different levels of defenses.

Object Relations

The figures in the stories represent the subject (the hero or identification figure) and other important figures in his or her life, such as parents, children, same-sex peers, love objects, siblings, and sometimes others. Attitudes toward, and relationships with, parental figures are usually seen in cards that show older and younger figures together, such as 2, 5, 6BM, 7BM, 7GF, 12F, and sometimes 8BM, 6GF, and 12M (Rapaport et al., 1968). Subjects usually identify with the younger-looking subjects on these cards because parental figures remain so significant in the subject's psychological world (Rapaport et al., 1968). Relationships with sexual partners are usually revealed in cards 4, 10, 13MF, and sometimes 5, 15, 17GF, 3GF, and 6GF (Rapaport et al., 1968).

The examiner should look at the relationships in the stories as depictions of the subject's own tendencies in relationships. To what extent are the relationships free of maladaptive elements more appropriate to childhood situations than present ones? Are relations characterized by unresolved conflicts, hostility, immaturity, or sadomasochism? Are relations gratifying to adult sexual, aggressive, and ego needs? Does the hero generally react to others with submission, autonomy, empathy, discomfort, enthusiasm, conflict, or noncompliance? What are the hero's emotional reactions to others? How does the hero anticipate others will treat him? The most pathological situation is a protocol that depicts a complete absence of social relations.

Conception of the Environment

Through the attitudes and encounters of the hero, the examiner can look at the subject's view of the world. This is because the subject's memories of the past influence his or her future expectations and color his or her interpretation of card stimuli. One should keep in mind such questions as the following: Does the outside world foster the hero's development or hinder his or her growth? Does the environment act as an obstacle or facilitator of the hero's goals? Is it friendly or hostile? Is the hero comfortable in his or her environment or in conflict with it? Look for what forms environmental obstacles take (such as other people), their frequency, and their strength.

Outcome of the Story

How the subject's stories are resolved reveals potentially important information about the subject. Degree of optimism or pessimism is demonstrated by the degree to which the stories have happy or unhappy endings. Reality testing and fantasy living are revealed by the appropriateness of the endings that, not atypically, have wish-fulfilling components. Sense of competence is shown by how successful the hero is in terms of reaching his or her goals, fulfilling his or her needs, and resolving conflict.

When interpreting content of the TAT, the examiner should weigh heavily the degree to which the story is consistent with the card stimuli. This can be done by comparison to norms, and to a lesser degree by relying on the examiner's own experience and apperception. Because there are thought to be three contributors to the response—the card stimulus, the testing environment, and the subject's inner world and experiences— the less the stimulus seems to contribute, the more the other two components are likely adding. Karon (1981) has suggested that the less the response "fits" the card, the more meaningful it probably is; that is, the more idiographic information it provides. Therefore, the more projection that seems to be taking place, the more the response should be weighed during interpretation.

In the preceding section, interpretation of story content was discussed primarily from the standpoint of idiographic interpretation, but normative comparison for these areas is also appropriate and desirable to put responses in context. The content of responses ranges from stereotypical to original, and is usually a mix, somewhere in between. A record that shows the ability to see things as others commonly see them and the ability to be creative demonstrates good ego-functioning of the subject. In general, stimuli to which subjects react with blatantly discordant responses and infrequent themes are likely to have personal meaning for the subject and deserve additional attention in interpretation.

Story Structure

In addition to the actual content of TAT stories being an indicator of a subject's personality, the structure, or the manner in which the stories are told, also yields much material for interpretation. The following section will describe various aspects of the storytelling the examiner may find useful to consider.

The basic tone of a story should be analyzed for underlying feelings, assumptions, and optimism or pessimism. The psychologist can use the degree to which the stories exemplify logical thinking as reflections of the subject's thought processes. The degree to which the stories conform with reality may indicate if psychoticism is present. Because the TAT responses are examples of the extent to which the subject is able to solve novel problems, the integrity and cohesiveness of a story should be viewed as indicators of the subject's ego-functioning. The subject's ability to tell appropriate stories with an appropriate amount of distance from the stories reflects how well the subject is able to function.

The examiner should note any unusual use of language by the subject. Extent of usage of adjectives, adverbs, multisyllabic words, and compound and complex sentences can be used to approximate the subject's level of intelligence (Stein, 1981). Poor grammar may indicate low education, or, if inconsistent across cards, it may reveal anxiety in reaction to a particular stimulus. Profanity may indicate, among other possibilities, poor impulse control, aggression toward the examiner, or disinhibition.

A subject's treatment of time periods (past, present, future) should be considered during interpretation. The proportion of time spent on each time period may indicate which period in time is most influential in the subject's life. Note when significant events take place; if any time periods are avoided; and expressed attitudes toward the past, present, and future. Is the future dreaded? Is the past seen as "the good old days"? This may be particularly relevant if the subject is currently going through a life transition, such as getting married or retiring.

The examiner should note which objects (that are relatively salient in the TAT pictures) are overlooked by the subject; these are called *omissions*. Omissions usually indicate that the ignored object is disturbing to the subject, and interpretation can speak to the subject's anxiety or conflict. The most extreme omission is complete rejection of the card. According to Rapaport et al. (1968), different omissions indicate different degrees of meaningfulness, depending on the degree of salience or ambiguity of the card. For example, a story ignoring the nude female figure on card 13MF would be more noteworthy than omitting the toy/keys/gun on card 3BM. The examiner should also check the degree to which the omission is common or unusual by comparison to norms.

On the other hand, subjects may include objects in their stories that are not in the picture cards. These are called *additions* and are far less frequent than *omissions*. These are always significant because they are pure projections, rather than a mixture of the stimulus and the subject's inner world. Additions may reflect wishes or fears. Much attention to a particular detail, even if not an addition, reveals preoccupation with the topic or a tendency toward obsessive thinking. Omissions and additions can occur in combination.

Being presented with a series of cards to respond to is comparable to facing consecutive events in daily life. By looking at the various stories told in sequence, the examiner is privy to the manner in which the subject reacts after various emotions are evoked. For example, after telling a stressful story in which the hero is attacked, does the next story speak of comfort in another's arms? Or does the hero in the next story experience an even more terrible encounter? Looking at the TAT stories in relation to the ones before and after them is called *sequence analysis*. This gives an indication of the subject's defenses, or reactions to stress.

The subject's defenses can also be revealed in unusual types of story structure; for example, responding with short descriptions of the pictures rather than stories, comments on pictures themselves (e.g., that they are out of date), or excessively detailed stories. The examiner should attempt to discern the type of defense used, and the adequacy of the defenses in warding off anxiety or depression, possibly by looking at the response to the following card and by observing the subject's behavior and nonverbal communication. Defenses that interfere with performing the TAT assessment may be viewed as inconsistent with adaptive functioning. For example, avoidance (possibly a defense against expression of anger) that prevents the subject from making up stories on the TAT may also be interfering with the subject's communication in personal relationships in life outside the testing situation.

The length and timing of stories should be considered indicators of subject conflict or preoccupation. The average story is 100 words told in about 3 minutes, and is begun after the stimulus card is presented for approximately 20 seconds (Rapaport et al., 1968). Significant deviations from these averages may point the examiner to potential areas of concern. The examiner should look for inter- and intra-individual inconsistencies (Rapaport et al.). Inter-individual inconsistencies (nomothetic) include patterns that consistently differ from average. These may reveal stable characteristics of the subject. For example, consistently quick response times may indicate impulsiveness, while long pauses may demonstrate defensiveness or slow cognitive processing. Intra-individual inconsistencies refer to differences in response compared to other stories by the same subject. For example, a particularly long story may reveal an area of preoccupation. When the psychologist notes to which cards these deviations occur, interpretations can take these exceptions into account.

Test Behavior Observations

The subject's behavior during testing is assumed to reflect his or her thoughts, feelings, and anxieties evoked in response to the testing situation and various card stimuli. Accordingly, by carefully observing the subject's nonverbal and verbal behavior, valuable information may be obtained regarding the subject's reactions to the various situations depicted in the cards, and the testing situation itself.

The quality of the subject's interaction with the examiner can be regarded as a sample of his or her interpersonal relations in general. The attitude toward the examiner, the amount of eye contact, friendliness, and appropriateness of the interaction should all be noted and used as corroborative evidence for patterns noticed in the story content.

Comments outside of the TAT stories should be considered material for interpretation. Statements of self-denigration or self-doubt, such as "Oh, I won't be good at this, I'm not creative," reflect the subject's view of his or her own competence. Subjects often verbalize their reactions to particular cards. For example, they may state whether they like or dislike the scenes, whether they are relevant or irrelevant to their own lives, and if they consider the pictures dated. Such comments can be considered defensive statements, because the subject is basically avoiding creating a story. In addition, declaring that the pictures are irrelevant or old-fashioned is a way of distancing oneself from the stories. This is an indication that the particular stimulus causes anxiety in the subject, or that unacceptable feelings or drives are threatening to surface in response to that card.

Subjects may also demonstrate their anxiety in response to the stimulus through nonverbal behavior. The examiner should take careful note of when the subject blushes, bites his or her nails, seems restless, smiles, frowns, exhibits mannerisms, alters fluency of speech, changes affect, and so on because these often indicate areas of conflict for the subject. It should be kept in mind that words may have different meanings depending on the tone with which they are delivered. Of particular note is when a subject's words and the emotionality behind the words seem to convey conflicting messages. For example, "He really loves his parents!" spoken with a cynical ring may inform the examiner that some conflict exists. Perhaps the subject hates his parents, perhaps the subject harbors guilt about his feelings toward his parents; the particular interpretation should be based on the context of the statement in terms of background information and other test responses.

Perhaps one of the clearest ways to obtain information about the subject is by observing the degree to which the subject complies with the given instructions to tell a story, including what is happening, what led up to it, what the characters are thinking and feeling, and how it all turned out. The most common omissions are thoughts and feelings of the stimulus characters (Rapaport et al., 1968). Compliance with instructions reflects the personality organization and general adequacy of functioning of the subject (Dana, 1985). The examiner should note the cards for which the subject gave an incomplete response, and which questions (e.g., what the characters are thinking, feeling, the outcome) are omitted. It also should be recorded if compliance was obtained through prompting by the examiner.

Noncompliance with instructions ordinarily reflects an inability to do so. According to Rapaport et al. (1968), failure to comply with particular instructions usually points up areas of conflict for the subject. It usually indicates that the material that would have been revealed had the instructions been followed would have been intolerable for the subject. It is cautioned that omissions on one card alone should not be overinterpreted and that patterns of noncompliance are far more meaningful. The opposite of noncompliance—strict adherence to instructions—such as the subject telling every story in the following pattern: "They are . . . what led up to it was . . . she is thinking . . . she is feeling . . . it ends up that . . . " may reflect a rigidity and compulsive need for structure, and possible obsessive tendencies.

☐ Rules and Cautions in Interpretation

Examiners should keep the following guidelines in mind when interpreting TAT stories. They will aid examiners in making interpretations that come validly from the data. These guidelines are based on ones presented in a previous book by the present authors concerning the Rorschach Technique (Aronow et al., 1994).

Be Conservative in Interpretation

Examiners should be cautious rather than bold when interpreting TAT stories. When in doubt about an interpretation, the examiner should prefer to err on the side of conservatism, rather than going out on a limb. It is better not to say anything than to say something that is invalid about the subject. Related to this guideline about being conservative in interpretation is the preference to err on the side of health rather than to err on the side of pathology. Essentially, be careful not to go beyond the data when making statements about an individual.

Use Caution when Interpreting Responses with Uncertain Referents

Sometimes it will not be clear whom the subject is referring to when creating characters in TAT stories. For example, if a young female subject describes a young male figure acting in a destructive manner, it may not be clear if the subject views men in general as aggressive, views young men as aggressive, or is projecting her ego-dystonic aggression onto someone of the opposite gender as an attempt at distancing herself from unacceptable proclivities. When the examiner cannot clarify these uncertainties by looking at the subject's other responses, the examiner should refrain from interpreting such material.

Attempt to Disentangle the Projective from the Nonprojective

TAT responses are a blend of objective description of the card stimuli, typical reactions, and projection of more individualized meaning. When interpreting the stories, the examiner should tease apart what aspects of the responses are reflections of which sources. Comparison to normative responses and clinical experience is useful to this end. In general, one should more readily interpret aspects of responses that come from the subject's own inner world than aspects that are more consistent with responses of others and the card stimuli.

Be Aware of Your Own Projection and Blind Spots

The examiner should be attentive to patterns in his or her own interpretation across subjects. If the examiner finds that he or she tends to describe the psychodynamics of a variety of diverse subjects in a similar manner, and particularly in a manner consistent with his or her own psychodynamics, it is possible that the examiner is projecting his or her personality into the interpretation. The opposite may also occur, where the examiner observes that certain themes of interpretation are completely absent in his or her interpretations of many records. In this case, a blindness to certain areas of psychodynamics may exist. Clinicians are encouraged to become as self-aware as possible in order to minimize such difficulties. Personal therapy is useful in this regard.

Attend to Indicators of Heavy Dynamic Loading

Take note of characteristics of responses that tend to have high personal meaning for the subject, including originality, change in volume of speech, increase or decrease of defensive behavior, show of emotion, imaginativeness, repetition, and change in nonverbal behavior, among others.

Rely on a Confluence of Data

Rather than attaching too much significance to any one response, examiners should look for corroboration among stories, and among different areas of interpretation (content, structure, and behavior observations). Interpretations made with this guideline in mind are likely to be more reliable and valid. Occasionally, however, there are exceptions where a single response or behavior is so striking that it warrants interpretation based on it alone. In these cases, it is appropriate to do so, qualifying the tentativeness of the interpretation and mentioning the isolated nature of the response.

The rule of using a *confluence of data* for interpretation can optimally be served by administering the TAT as a part of a test battery, rather than in isolation. If a battery is used, then hypotheses based on TAT data can also be supported or negated by responses coming from other tests that, together, may create a more complete and accurate portrait of the subject.

Consider the Subject's History

The more comprehensive a history the examiner has of the subject, the more effective will be the idiographic interpretation of the test data. It is helpful to know the subject's age, marital status, education, family configuration, occupation, psychiatric history, and significant life events and stressors. To interpret TAT stories without such information is "blind analysis." We recommend that taking a reasonably comprehensive history be part of the assessment process. However, on occasion it is not possible to obtain much background information. In these instances, one can offer a legitimate TAT interpretation, but one should certainly be aware that it is at a far more conjectural level.

Obtain Feedback from Other Professionals

Periodically, an examiner should ask other professionals for feedback about the accuracy of his or her interpretation of test material. For example, the examiner might approach the psychotherapist of a subject (if this was agreed upon during informed consent) to see if interpretations fit with what the therapist sees. The examiner could also ask any other professional experienced in TAT interpretation for reliability checks. Obtaining feedback can help the examiner avoid misinterpretations and help the psychologist become aware of his or her own blindspots.

Consider the Context

Psychologists should take into account the context in which the testing took place. What environmental factors may have influenced the responses? Was the assessment conducted in a hospital? Was it done by a stranger? Was the room comfortable? The potential impact of these factors should be considered.

Use the Appropriate Degree of Generalization

The degree of generalization influences the validity of your conclusions. The more specific the conclusion, the more difficult it is to confirm and the easier it is to invalidate. The more general the conclusion, the more likely it is to be valid (Piotrowski, 1950). For example, if a subject tells a story in which a boy smashes the violin his parents make him play, the interpretation would be more likely to be correct if it said, "The subject may have aggressive tendencies," than if it said, "The subject breaks objects when his parents act controlling."

Beginners tend to interpret stories too literally (Stein, 1981). For example, on card 7GF, the subject tells a story in which the little girl does not want to stay inside and listen to the book being read, but wishes she were outside taking a walk in the sunshine. One should not automatically assume the subject prefers walking to reading, unless evidence from other stories supports this. Instead, one may interpret that the subject is dissatisfied with her current activities and wishes for change. The feelings and attitudes expressed by the subject are typically more valid than the particular stimulus objects mentioned because the feelings are more likely projections, as opposed to the stimulus objects that are more objectively presented in the pictures.

Beware of First Impressions

Psychologists should take care not to unduly weight the first few stories read. It is poor practice to form hypotheses from the first few cards and use later stories to gather confirming evidence while ignoring disconfirming evidence. All cards should be read for possible new hypotheses and all data should be taken into consideration (Zubin et al., 1965). Similarly, psychologists should not be unduly swayed by the initial appearance and behavior of the subject.

Take Developmental Status into Account in Interpreting Children's TAT Stories

When interpreting TAT stories told by children, one must consider the child's age, developmental status, and verbal ability. Younger age is generally associated with lower normative impulse control, less sophisticated and proper language, and less maturity in peer relations. Fantasy living is more acceptable in children than in adults. Overall, the range of what is considered "normal" is somewhat greater in children. Examiners more familiar with assessing adults should be careful not to overpathologize the responses of children and should remember that adult norms are inappropriate for assessing the commonality of responses in children. With children, it is even more important to consider the testing context and behavioral observations.

Demonstrate Cultural Sensitivity

Assessors are ethically obligated to consider cultural issues in interpretation of test material. Before embarking on any type of testing, examiners should be familiar with the Human Differences Standard of the APA's ethics code. Examiners should "obtain the training, experience, consultation, or supervision necessary to ensure the competence of their services" where human differences significantly affect the psychologist's work (Canter, Bennett, Jones, & Nagy, 1994, p. 39). This maximizes the chance that responses will be considered in cultural context (Dana, 1985).

Method of Interpretation

The following is our recommended procedure for interpreting TAT test material. In summary, interpretation is based on verbatim recording, summarizing the stories, determining which aspects of the stories are most significant, organizing the material by areas of subject personality, comparison to norms, making hypotheses, and discerning meaning about the individual subject.

1. Read the stories, highlighting or underlining significant material. This may include such aspects as introduced objects, emotional language, unusual use of language, and descriptions of relationships. It should be

remembered that the TAT is best used as an instrument to assess the psychodynamics of interpersonal relationships.

2. Write summary statements of the main themes for each story. Notes may be made in the margins regarding tentative interpretive hypotheses.

3. Note which cards (which types of stimuli) evoked which reactions (e.g., anxiety, comfort, anger) in the subject.

4. Look over a list of common areas to interpret, such as the ones presented in this chapter, to avoid leaving out important indicators of personality.

5. Compare to norms and note unusual occurrences or lack of them.

6. Looking at highlighted material, main themes, story structure, and behavioral observations, note repetitions of themes, conflicts, and reactions.

7. Consider the subject's age, sex, culture, family structure, and occupation. Organize material, make sense of the patterns noted, and develop hypotheses. In interpretation of material, use common sense, life experience, and psychological training (Karon, 1981).

8. Integrate different aspects of the individual's personality into a meaningful picture that can be described in a report.

CHAPTER

Stimulus Characteristics of the TAT Cards

In order to interpret projective material, it is essential to be able to disentangle what is projective from what is an accurate description of the stimulus. Some degree of familiarity with what is typically described by subjects on particular TAT cards is, therefore, quite helpful to the practicing clinician. As Zubin (1949) stated, "It is clear that . . . the stimulus itself needs much more clarification before we can differentiate that which inheres in the stimulus from that which inheres in the responder himself" (p. 18). It is strongly recommended that the aspiring clinician become acquainted with what is known about the TAT card stimulus characteristics.

Eron (1950) carried out a very comprehensive study on the stimulus values of TAT cards using male subjects. In this study, approximately 3,000 TAT stories contributed by 150 male veterans were analyzed. The subject pool included 50 college students, 25 nonhospitalized "psychoneurotics," 25 hospitalized psychoneurotics, 25 hospitalized schizophrenics, and 25 miscellaneous neuropsychiatric patients.

One major finding of this study was that the preponderance of stories told by all subjects on the TAT was sad. This corresponds with commonsense views of the TAT cards and strongly suggests that negatively toned stories should be interpreted very conservatively. However, there was also a tendency on the part of the more normal subjects to give the stories a relatively happy ending—suggesting, perhaps, that the ending of the stories is a critical point. Fewer individuals in the hospitalized groups gave extreme outcomes as well.

Eron (1950) also found that sex misidentifications of the figures were common, with no particular differences evident between the normal and the clinical groups. The overinterpretation of sex misidentifications is, thus, something to be avoided. However, Eron found that misidentifications involving variables other than sex were more common in the general hospital group. Other differences that were found include the normal subjects offering more themes of belongingness and also of rumination.

In a table, Eron (1950) reported on the "stimulatory value" of TAT cards (i.e., the number of themes elicited by the cards). The rank ordering was as follows (from most themes to least themes elicited): 13MF, 20, 18BM, 6BM, 3BM, 4, 12M, 15, 7BM, 10, 17BM, 8BM, 9BM, 14, 5, 2, 1, 19, 11, and 16. However, even the least stimulatory card, card 16 (the blank card), elicited fully 199 themes.

In 1953, Eron published a study utilizing female subjects via college students and a group of pregnant women. Eron again reported the most common themes for TAT cards.

In a 1972 study, Murstein investigated the stimulus pull of TAT cards for a group of introductory psychology college students. In this study, Murstein found that the students' stories tended to be predominantly sad in terms of what is happening and why it is happening, but that the stories tended to have happy endings. Considerable variation was found among the cards. Thus, cards 2, 8GF, 11, and 14 were found to be predominantly neutral for the "what" and "why" categories, whereas 3BM, 3GF, 13MF, and 18BM were highly negative in these respects. Cards 8BM, 10, 12M, and 18GF were predominantly positive.

Goldfried and Zax (1965) used semantic differential ratings of male and female college students to describe the characteristics of the TAT cards (with the exception of the blank card).

In a 1962 study, Weisskopf-Joelson and Foster tested whether having humans or animals as the protagonists in pictures produced greater emotional productivity in stories, and also whether colored or black and white cards produced more productive stories. In this study, kindergarten students were the subjects. Modifications of four CAT cards were made to produce the human and color conditions.

The authors found that neither the human or animal variable nor the color variable affected the emotional productivity of the cards. However, there was a tendency for subjects with low *transcendence* scores to tell their most productive stories to animal and black and white pictures, with high transcendence subjects tending to tell their most productive stories to chromatic pictures. Transcendence refers to going beyond the obvious stimulus qualities of the cards.

In a 1950 study, Weisskopf found that college-age subjects are significantly more productive when responding to pictures about parent-child relationships and about heterosexual relationships among contemporaries than to pictures about other topics.

The following is a summary of the general appearance of the TAT cards, what in our experience are common themes, and what the research literature seems to indicate about them.

Card 1

This card presents a picture of a boy staring in contemplation at a violin. Morgan (1995) indicates that this card had its origin in a drawing by Christiana Morgan based on a photograph of the violinist, Yehudi Menuhin, as a child.

Bellak and Abrams (1997) have characterized this card as the most useful in the entire TAT. Common themes elicited include those of achievement, fear of failure, and sometimes a conflict between parental demands and the desires of the boy in the picture.

Eron's 1950 study found that for males the most frequent story is neutral to moderately sad. The most frequent outcome is happy. When there is an emotional shift from the body of the story to the outcome, more subjects shift to happier rather than sadder conclusions. The three most frequent themes, according to this study, are aspiration, parental pressure, and belongingness.

In Eron's 1953 study with female subjects, the most common themes for this card were parental pressure, occupational concern, and aspiration. The semantic differential study of Goldfried and Zax (1965) found that males and females tended to view this card as passive and somewhat sad.

Card 2

This card presents a rural scene with a young girl in the foreground holding a book, a pregnant woman watching, and a man laboring in a field in the background. According to Morgan (1995), this card had its origin in a painting done by the artist, Kroll.

In our experience, the most common theme is one of the young girl desiring to continue her education and leave the farm, contrary to the desires of the family. Sometimes there is an alliance described between certain members of the family against other members that can be revealing.

Eron's 1950 study found that for males the most frequent story is moderately happy and the most frequent outcome is happy. More subjects shift to happy rather than sad conclusions. The three most frequent themes are occupational concern, aspiration, and economic pressure.

Eron's (1953) study with females found that the three most common themes are aspiration, occupational concern, and parental pressure. The semantic differential study found this card to be lacking in strong stimulus quality.

Card 3BM

A figure (male or female?) is huddled on the floor with an indistinct object (keys? a gun?) on the floor. Morgan (1995) indicated that this card represents a drawing by Christiana Morgan based on an existing photograph.

In our experience, this card strongly brings forth depressive themes, such as suicide or depression over loss of a relationship. Themes of drug abuse may result from the object on the floor being perceived as a needle.

Eron's (1950) study found that with male subjects, the preponderance of stories are moderately to very sad. The most frequent outcome is moderately happy. About half of all subjects shift to happier conclusions. The three most frequent themes are suicide, parental pressure, and behavior disorder.

Semantic differential studies of this card point to a strong negative quality, with it being perceived as quite sad, hopeless, and unpleasant. The examiner should be wary of overinterpreting negative stories told to Card 3BM.

Card 3GF

This card portrays a female figure standing next to an open door. One hand is clutching her face, which is downcast. Morgan (1995) has little to say about the provenance of this card. In our experience this card, like 3BM, strongly elicits depressive themes. Eron's (1953) study with female subjects found the most common themes for this card involved the death or illness of a child, pressures from a partner, or an unrequited female partner.

The semantic differential studies with 3GF come out similar to those with 3BM, with sadness, hopelessness, and unpleasantness prominent. As with 3BM, the examiner should be careful not to overinterpret negatively tinged stories to this card.

Card 4

This card portrays a woman grabbing the shoulders of a man while the man is turning away from her. There is a distant picture of another woman undressing in the background. Morgan (1995) indicated that this card comes from a color illustration.

In our experience, the woman is usually perceived as trying to restrain the man from hostile action or there is a love triangle involving the figure in the background. Eron's (1950) study with male subjects found that emotional tone ratings are neutral to mildly negative. The most frequent outcome is moderately happy. Only rarely will subjects shift to sadder conclusions. The three most frequent themes are pressure from a partner, succorance from a partner, and competition.

The Eron (1953) study with females found the most common themes to be succorance from a partner, departure from partner, and nurturance to partner. The semantic differential ratings of this card paint strong and definite reactions to it, involving the card being described as impulsive, aggressive, and dangerous.

The nature of how male and female relations are seen can be portrayed very graphically on this card.

Card 5

This card portrays an older woman looking into a room from the doorway with a look (of surprise?) on her face. Morgan (1995) reports that this drawing was originally done by Christiana Morgan.

Feelings involving the mother are often elicited by this card. Where she catches the child misbehaving, it is interesting to note how she handles it—Is she understanding? Does she invoke guilt?

Eron's (1950) study found that the most frequent story to this card is neutral to moderately negative, with the most frequent outcome neutral. The three most frequent themes involved curiosity, pressure from parents, and illicit sex.

Eron's (1953) study with female subjects found the three most frequent themes to be curiosity, parental pressure, and concern on the part of the parent. Semantic differential study of this card yields ambiguous results.

Card 6BM

This card portrays an older woman in interaction with a somewhat younger male. Morgan (1995) reports that this picture likewise had its origin in a drawing by Christiana Morgan.

In our experience, common themes involve bringing the mother bad news or informing the mother that he (the son) is leaving or moving out. Eron's (1950) study found that most stories to this picture are sad, with neutral stories rare. More than half the subjects shift to happier conclusions. The three most frequent themes are pressure from parents, departure from parents, and marriage of a child. Both male and female subjects in the semantic differential study viewed this card as sad and unpleasant.

This card is often referred to as the *mother card* for male subjects. It is thus interesting to note the complexity of feelings between the male and female figures, whether she is designated as his mother or not.

Card 6GF

A younger woman is sitting down and turning to a somewhat older man with a pipe who is behind her. Morgan (1995) indicates that this card originated in a black and white illustration. In our experience, this card most typically involves the man suggesting something to the woman, whether sexual or otherwise.

The Eron (1953) study using female subjects found that the three most common themes for this card were pressure from partner, fear or worry, and ordinary activity. The semantic differential study found males and females viewed this card differently, with males viewing the card as only slightly aggressive and impulsive; but females viewing it as quite aggressive, and slightly impulsive, unpleasant, dangerous, severe, and sexy. The theme of a sexual advance is thus suggested, at least for female subjects.

This card has been described as the *father card* for female subjects; however, the similarity in ages between the people pictured renders this approach somewhat questionable. The card may thus be more of a reflection of heterosexual relations generally. Thus, is the interaction positive, or is the male regarded, for instance, as inappropriately intrusive?

Card 7BM

This card features an older man looking at a younger man who is not returning the look. Morgan (1995) has little to say of the origin of this card. In our experience, this card typically elicits stories of an older man giving advice to a younger man. The 1950 Eron study found that the most frequent story to this card is neutral to moderately sad. The most frequent outcome is moderately happy. There are many shifts to happier conclusions. The three most frequent themes seen were succorance from a parent, pressure from parents, and occupational concern.

Semantic differential study of this card suggested an ambiguous appearance. This card has been described as the father card for male subjects and in our experience is successful in eliciting feelings toward the father and other male authority figures.

Card 7GF

A young girl is seated, holding a doll(?) while a woman is reading a book to her. The young girl is staring into space. According to Morgan (1995), this card originated in a black and white reproduction of a painting.

In our experience, this card does stimulate themes of mother–daughter interactions. The 1953 Eron study with female subjects found that the three most common themes elicited were parental pressure, facts of life, and that a sibling is coming.

Semantic differential study of this card finds it being described as passive and safe. This card has been referred to as the mother card for female subjects and is apparently successful in that respect. Psychologists should be aware of the feelings between mother and daughter that are being elicited.

Card 8BM

This card depicts a young boy in the foreground with an operation taking place behind him. The barrel of a rifle is visible at one side. According to Morgan (1995), this card had its origin in an illustration that accompanied a short story and pictured an emergency appendectomy.

In our experience, common stories to this card center around ambition or an operation scene. In Eron's (1950) study, it was reported that about half of all stories were moderately sad, with about half of all outcomes moderately happy. There is a frequent shift to the happy direction. The three most common themes seen were aspiration, war, and death or illness of a parent. The semantic differential study suggested a somewhat ambiguous stimulus.

It is not unusual for Oedipal conflicts to be seen on this card, with the subject identifying with the adolescent boy. How these conflicts are played out can be quite interesting.

Card 8GF

A woman is seated and staring off into space. According to Morgan (1995), this card originated as an oil painting currently at the Metropolitan Museum of Art in New York City.

In our experience, this is a vague card that does not yield particularly interesting stories. The three most common themes reported in Eron's (1953) study of female subjects involved happy reminiscence, aspiration, and occupational concern. The semantic differential study generally found a positive tone for this card.

Card 9BM

This card depicts four men lying down against each other in a field. According to Morgan (1995), this card originated as a photograph with Western-style clothing more prominent in the photograph.

In our experience, this card typically elicits stories involving a hobo theme. Eron (1950) found that the most frequent story is neutral in tone. The three most frequent themes were found to be retirement, exhaustion, and vacillation. The semantic differential study suggested a lack of specific stimulus qualities.

Card 9GF

This card features two female figures. One of them is standing behind a tree, watching the other run along a beach. According to Morgan (1995), this card originated as an illustration to accompany a serialized novel.

In our experience, this card usually elicits a story involving conflict between the two female figures, usually over a man. Eron's (1953) study with female subjects found that the three most common themes involved escape from a perilous environment, curiosity, and jealousy. The semantic differential study found both male and female subjects viewing this as an unhappy card. Themes of female peer competition are often seen on this card. The card may also tend to elicit paranoid themes because of the element of the one woman being observed.

Card 10

Seen on this card is a young woman's head leaning against a man's shoulder. Morgan indicates that this card originated as a photograph. In our experience, this card usually involves a story about a heterosexual relationship. Eron (1950) found that the most frequent outcome for this story was moderately happy. The three most frequent themes seen were contentment with a partner, nurturance to a partner, and departure from a partner.

The Eron (1953) study with female subjects found that the three most common themes were contentment, death or illness of a child, and nurturance to a partner. The semantic differential study found this to be rated as one of the happiest cards.

The quality and fabric of heterosexual relationships are often clearly seen in stories to this card. If both parties are indicated to be male, this may be indicative of homosexual orientation in male subjects.

Card 11

This card presents a picture of a road by a chasm between high cliffs—on one side is the head and neck of a dragon(?). This card stems from a painting by the 19th-century Swiss artist, Bocklin (Morgan, 1995).

In our experience, this is one of the less useful and less frequently used of the TAT cards. Eron (1950) found that the most frequent story for this card is moderately sad, with the most frequent outcome neutral. The three most frequent themes were aggression from an impersonal source, escape from peril, and aggression from a peer.

The Eron (1953) study with female subjects found the three most common themes to be aggression from the environment, escape from a perilous environment, and fear or worry. The semantic differential study indicated a connotation of fear for this card.

Card 12M

This card depicts a man with his hand raised and a boy lying down with his eyes closed. Morgan (1995) indicated only that this card appeared with some variations in earlier scenes of the TAT.

Eron (1950) found that the most frequent story for this card is moderately sad, with stories rarely happy. The three most frequent themes were hypnotism, religion, and illness or death of the central character. The semantic differential study suggested few strong stimulus characteristics for this card.

In our experience, this card can be particularly useful in elucidating a patient's possible reaction to psychotherapy, that is, the nature of the relationship that he or she is likely to establish in therapy.

Card 12F

This represents a portrait of a young woman with a weird old woman grimacing in the background. Morgan (1995) described this card as originating in a drawing by Christiana Morgan based on a painting by the English artist, Augustus Jolin.

It is not uncommon for the older woman to have very negative qualities ascribed to her, and often be described as a stepmother or mother-in-law. This may, in fact, be a disguise for feelings toward the mother.

Eron's (1953) study found that the three most frequent themes with female subjects were found to be disappointment in a parent, parental pressure, and succorance from a parent. The semantic differential study suggested a neutral or sad emotional tone for female subjects.

Card 12BG

This card displays a rowboat drawn upon the bank of a woodland stream. Morgan (1995) described this card as originating in a photograph by a well-known photographer. The semantic differential study indicated that this card has strong and pleasant connotations for both male and female subjects. Healthy subjects typically describe a happy, peaceful scene. Sometimes themes of loneliness and even suicide are found in less healthy test records.

Card 13MF

This card depicts a male with his head buried in his arm, with an unclad woman lying (lifeless?) behind him in the bed. This card is simply described by Morgan (1995) as being similar to earlier editions of the TAT cards.

In our experience, this card presents a strong stimulus for both sexual and aggressive themes for subjects. If sex and aggression are not present in the story, this may suggest strong uses of denial. Eron (1950) found that the great preponderance of subjects' stories were sad. The three most frequent themes seen were death or illness of partner, guilt and remorse, and illicit sex.

In Eron's (1953) study with female subjects, the three most common themes were death or illness of a female partner, guilt, and aggression from the male partner. The semantic differential study found significant differences between male and female subjects, with the females attributing more phobic and dangerous characteristics to the scene.

Card 13B

This card displays a young boy sitting on the doorstep of a log cabin. According to Morgan (1995), this card has its origin in a photograph entitled, "Mr. Abe Lincoln, Jr." The cropped print of it by Murray focuses more attention on the child.

In our experience, how childhood is viewed is often revealed in stories to this card and, sometimes, themes of loneliness are seen. The semantic differential study of this card indicates that the stimulus characteristics are not strong or pronounced.

Card 13G

This card depicts a little girl climbing a winding flight of steps. Morgan (1995) indicated that this card originated as a photo of the photographer's wife, who was petite.

Like the previous card, themes of childhood and loneliness are found in stories to this card. The semantic differential study indicates no strong stimulus properties for this card.

Card 14

This card shows a person's silhouette against a window. Morgan (1995) indicated that this card was an original drawing by Christiana Morgan. In our experience, this card is sensitive to themes of contemplation, sometimes burglary, and also themes of depression and possibly suicidal ideation. Eron (1950) found that the three most frequent themes of male subjects were curiosity, aspiration, and happy reminiscence. In the 1953 Eron study of female subjects, the three most common themes were aspiration, ordinary activity, and occupational concern. The semantic differential study generally found this card viewed in a positive manner.

Card 15

This card portrays a gaunt man with clenched hands standing among grave stones. Morgan (1995) indicated that this card originated in a woodcut print by an American illustrator.

Eron (1950) reported that the most frequent story to this card was extremely sad, with the most frequent outcome sad. The three most common themes found were death or illness of a partner, religion, and death or illness of a peer.

Eron (1953) found that among female subjects, the three most common themes were intra-aggression, religion, and death or illness of a female partner. A very sad quality was indicated in the semantic differential study of this card.

In our experience, this is not one of the more useful cards. It is so structured that it almost always produces death themes.

Card 16

This is the blank card in the series. For best results, it should be administered as the last in the series. Stories are highly variable—some are quite revealing, with others revealing little or nothing about the subject.

Eron (1950) found that the most frequent story is neutral in tone. The three most common themes were found to be favorable environment, war, and contentment with a partner.

Eron (1953) found that among female subjects, the three most common themes were parental contentment, aspiration, and aggression from the environment.

Card 17BM

This card shows a (naked?) man climbing a rope. This card is described by Morgan (1995) as a drawing by Thal based on an unfinished sketch by Daumier.

In our experience, frequent themes involve athletic events or escape from a dangerous situation. Because of the nudity, themes involving homosexual ideation may be obtained from latent homosexual male subjects.

Eron (1950) found that the most frequent story to this card was neutral to moderately happy. The three most frequent themes were self-esteem, exhibition, and competition with a peer. A neutral to moderately happy view of this card was suggested by the semantic differential study.

Card 17GF

This card shows a female figure leaning over a bridge's railing with tall buildings and small figures of men in the background. Morgan (1995) indicated that this card originated as a woodcut.

In our experience, this is not one of the more useful cards. An exception is that individuals may see the figure as contemplating or preparing to commit suicide by jumping off the bridge.

Eron (1953) found that among female subjects the three most common themes were suicide, ordinary activity, and curiosity. The semantic differential study found this card to be low in stimulus properties.

Card 18BM

This card shows a man being clutched from behind by three hands. Morgan (1995) indicated that this card originated in a drawing by Christiana Morgan.

Eron (1950) found that the most frequent story to this card is neutral to moderately happy. The three most frequent themes were found to be self-esteem, exhibition, and competition with a peer. A neutral to moderately happy tone for this card was suggested by the semantic differential study.

In our experience, drunkenness and attitudes toward it is a common theme for this card. Paranoid individuals may also react to it as representing an "attack from behind."

Card 18GF

This card displays a woman with her hands around the throat of another woman, with a flight of stairs seen. Morgan (1995) indicates that this image was redrawn by Thal, possibly from an earlier photograph.

Eron (1953) found that among female subjects, the three most common themes for this card were found to be succorance from a parent, parental pressure, and death or illness of a child. A negative valence for this card was suggested by the semantic differential study.

In our experience, hostile interactions with other female figures tend to be highlighted in stories to this card, whether Oedipal in nature or not.

Card 19

This card presents a "weird" picture of clouds over a snow-covered cabin. Morgan (1995) reported that this card is based on a watercolor painting that was done by a painter who, at the time, was suffering from severe depression and hallucinations.

In our experience, this is not one of the more useful cards. The Eron (1950) study found that the most frequent story to this card is neutral to moderately sad. The three most frequent themes seen were aggression from an impersonal source, contentment at home, and vacillation.

In the Eron (1953) study with female subjects, the three most common themes were aggression from the environment, contentment with a parent, and the supernatural. In the semantic differential study, females had a somewhat more negative impression of this card than did males.

Card 20

This card represents a somewhat hazy picture of a man leaning against a lamppost at night. Morgan (1995) indicated that this card had its origin in a photograph.

In our experience, a variety of stories can be elicited by this blot, including themes of loneliness, going on a date, or a sinister encounter. Eron (1950) found that with male subjects the most frequent story is moderately sad. The three most common themes seen were vacillation, economic pressure, and aggression from an impersonal source.

In the 1953 Eron study, the three most common themes were vacillation, loneliness, and aggression to the environment. No particular pattern was evident in semantic differential study of this card.

Research Findings

Research studies that have utilized the TAT are quite numerous. The present chapter will concern itself with areas that have been researched in some depth and have significant clinical relevance.

☐ Need for Achievement

David McClelland's need for achievement research has been one of the more famous and creative efforts in TAT research. McClelland and his co-workers somewhat narrowed Murray's definition of the nAch to, essentially, desire to do a good job; that is, to attain a standard of excellence (McClelland et al., 1953; McClelland, 1961a, 1961b).

McClelland used several TAT pictures, but also included stimuli specially designed to elicit nAch. Instructions were also often modified to enhance nAch. It should be noted that McClelland assumed that nAch is learned rather than innate. Further, McClelland found that nAch, as he measured it, did not correlate with subjects' own self-descriptions as to the strength of such a motive in themselves (McClelland, Koestner, & Weinberger, 1989; Spangler, 1992).

NAch has also been found to have biological correlates. Thus, the arousal of nAch has been shown to be related to the release of the antidiuretic hormone argine vasopressin (McClelland, 1995). This hormone enhances memory for the situations in which the subject is involved (McGaugh, 1990). It has been hypothesized that nAch-invoking situations (such as moderately challenging tasks) become incentives and consequently are rewarded with enhanced memory and learning of the behavior in question. McClelland and Pilon (1983) have suggested that scheduled infant feeding and strict toilet training are related to the development of nAch. With respect to the latter, McClelland has reasoned that if a young child is punished for relieving him- or herself at the wrong time, argine vasopressin will be released, associated with parental urgings to act more appropriately. Since such learning takes place very early, this might explain its persistence throughout life.

Much of McClelland's work has dealt with an even more narrow aspect of nAch, what might be referred to as nEAch, a need for economic achievement (usually an entrepreneurial type of achievement). McClelland's measures have been found to be rather good predictors of success in the business world (business perhaps representing an optimum middle ground between risk and incentive).

Thus, McClelland (1965) has demonstrated that college students scoring high in nAch are more likely to make their living in entrepreneurial occupations than those low in nAch (over a period of fourteen years). In addition, he has found that primitive tribes with folk tales high in nAch are more likely to contain entrepreneurs, and also that increases in achievement themes found in children's readers tend to precede increases in a nation's economic production (McClelland, 1961a).

McClelland and others have done some interesting research relating child-rearing techniques to nAch. For example, Winterbottom (1958) tested boys 8 to 10 years old for nAch, and related these data to their upbringing. Among other things, she found that mothers of boys low in nAch often made their sons' decisions for them and tended to restrict their behavior. In contrast, the mothers of high nAch boys expected more independence and self-reliance from their sons (e.g., make their own friends, do things for themselves). These mothers also displayed more of a tendency to reward their sons for such behavior with physical affection than did the mothers of boys with low nAch.

Studies of fathers of high nAch boys (see Birney, 1968) have found these fathers to be emotionally warmer toward these sons and to be more demanding of high achievement (though less directive of how the achievement is to be accomplished).

A major finding of McClelland and other authors has been that high nAch individuals prefer situations with a "middling" probability of success, seen in such situations as the distance children prefer to stand from the target in a ring-toss game (McClelland, 1958), and college subjects choosing geometrical puzzles with different degrees of difficulty (Weiner, 1970).

Studies of nAch have often been intertwined with a different, though related, motive—what has been called the *fear of failure* (FF). John Atkinson has been most identified with this body of research. Atkinson and co-workers (e.g., Atkinson and Feather, 1966) have actually developed mathematical formulae that combine nAch, FF, and the incentive value of the situation in predicting behavior. Atkinson has found that subjects with high nAch and low FF will gravitate toward "easy" tasks. Those with low nAch and high FF will prefer difficult tasks (presumably, the high FF subjects can blame failure on a difficult task on the task itself).

☐ Hostility and Aggression

A major focus of research with the TAT has been the measurement of hostility and aggression. For example, Megargee (1967) explored the relationship between hostility on the TAT and defensive inhibition. The hypothesis was that differences would be found between inhibited and uninhibited subjects when instructions suggested a hostile response, but would not be present without such suggestion. Less inhibited subjects were indeed found to have higher hostility scores than the more inhibited subjects, but only for female subjects. In addition, instructions to give hostile responses resulted in more hostile stories than did the neutral instructions, and the more the aggressive pull of the card, the higher the hostility score. These results again applied only for female subjects.

Sanford et al. (1943) found a relationship among middle-class subjects between high aggressive needs as seen on the TAT with low overt aggression. Using a lower-class sample, Mussen and Naylor (1954) predicted that high fantasy aggression on the TAT would indeed be predictive of overt aggression. This prediction was based on the authors' assumption that aggression is less frequently punished in lower-class settings. Using a delinquent population of teenagers and pre-teenagers, they did indeed find that high aggressiveness in TAT stories was predictive of aggressive behavior in the real world. Further, those boys who were shown less punishment press pertaining to aggressive needs in their stories were more likely to show overt aggression.

Weissman (1964), in a related study, compared four groups of adolescents: aggressive acting-out subjects in an institution, less aggressive acting-out subjects in an institution, high-school boys with no history of acting out, and high-school boys with a history of acting out. The number of aggressive TAT stories told was found to be a good predictor of acting-out behavior, as was the appearance of aggressive stories to nonaggressive cards. The best predictor of aggression was found to be the reaction time of the subjects.

Reznikoff and Dollin (1961) studied the relationship between aggressive stories to the TAT and the Edwards Social Desirability Scale. These authors found that high social desirability (S.D.) subjects were more likely to use covert than overt hostility.

James and Mosher (1967) studied aggression in TAT stories with reference to the stimulus pull of the cards. Working with Boy Scouts, they found that thematic aggression to cards high in such stimulus pull was related to overt aggressive behavior, but this was not the case for cards low in stimulus pull for aggression. Additionally, these authors found that there was a significant negative relationship between hostility guilt and aggressive stories given to cards with low aggressive pull. This study is important in that it suggests that, at least for the measurement of hostility and aggression potential, one would want to use cards of high relevance to aggression.

Hafner and Kaplan (1960) compared the ability of both the Rorschach Test and the TAT to measure overt and covert hostility. For the TAT, overt and covert hostility were found to be negatively related to each other. It was concluded that the TAT might be more sensitive than the Rorschach to the overt versus covert nature of hostility.

In an early study, Fisher and Hinds (1951) dealt with psychiatric patients and a normal control group. In this study, one of six comparisons reached significance, namely, suicidal schizophrenics were found to display more outward hostility than paranoid subjects.

In a 1957 investigation, Scodel and Lipetz contrasted three groups of schizophrenics on TAT hostility. The three groups were composed of nonviolent subjects, subjects who had displayed external violence, and suicidal subjects. No differences in TAT hostility were found.

Purcell (1956), in a very interesting study, investigated differences in various hostile aspects of TAT stories of three groups that differed in degree of antisocial behavior. The very antisocial subjects were found to display more direct and undisguised TAT hostility than the least antisocial subjects.

Haskin (1958) studied college students and psychiatric patients in terms of their TAT *realistic aggression* and *unrealistic aggression*. Realistic aggression was defined as socially acceptable, and an appropriate means of expression; unrealistic aggression was defined as inappropriate or punitive aggression, or aggression turned against the self. This author found that the normal students showed significantly more realistic aggression, while the patients displayed significantly more unrealistic aggression.

Haskell (1961) worked with hospitalized schizophrenic patients. With reference to the TAT, Haskell found that social history of aggression and nurses' ratings of aggression correlated significantly with TAT aggression, but therapist evaluation of aggression did not relate to TAT aggression.

Megargee and Cook (1967) studied the Holtzman Inkblot Technique and TAT protocols of 76 juvenile delinquents, with four TAT and five ink-blot aggressive content scales utilized. Eleven different criteria of overt aggression were used. Both inkblot and TAT content scales were found to be related to certain criteria. There was no indication that the inkblot scales tapped a "deeper" aspect of aggression. The authors suggested that the highly defensive nature of the sample may have clouded the results obtained.

In sum, while such a conclusion is somewhat controversial, the general results indicated that TAT aggression can, at least under certain circum-stances, predict overt aggression.

☐ Scoring of Defense Mechanisms

Phebe Cramer (1990) has put forward a well-detailed and subsequently well-validated manual for scoring defense mechanisms on the TAT. Three types of defenses are scored: Denial, Projection, and Identification. Denial is deemed to be the most primitive of the three, with Identification the least primitive. Each is coded on several levels, again ranging from the more primitive to the more sophisticated.

In a 1987 investigation, Cramer described a study in which children ranging in age from 5 to 15 showed a predicted progression with age from the most primitive defense mechanism in her system through the most sophisticated. In another study (Cramer, Blatt, & Ford, 1988) scores of inpatients on measures of psychological impairment and maturity were related to Cramer's TAT defense scoring in a manner that largely validated the developmental order of the three TAT-scored defenses.

Hibbard et al. (1994) contrasted college students with acute psychiatric patients. In this study, the psychiatric patients were found to use the more primitive defense mechanisms and also, within each defense mechanism, to use lower levels significantly more often than the college students.

Porcerelli, Thomas, Hibbard, and Cogan (1998) have worked with stu-dents of a large age range, from grade 2 through college freshmen. These authors found that as grade level increased, relative use of Denial and Projection decreased; as might be expected, use of Identification increased.

In a study that again supported the construct validity of Cramer's defense mechanism scoring system but that also suggested a complexity with respect to gender continuity of defensive style over time, Cramer and Block (1998) reevaluated the TAT defenses of subjects at age 23 who had previously been evaluated while in nursery school. In this study, it was found that there was continuity of defense use for male participants, but not for females. A variety of possible explanations for this discrepancy were discussed. It is nonetheless remarkable that Cramer was able to demonstrate continuity of TAT-measured defensive style over such a large amount of time, even for just the male subjects.

The studies discussed represent just a small percentage of those that have consistently supported the construct validity of Cramer's TAT scales of defense. These scales clearly represent a very promising area for future TAT research.

☐ Interpersonal Object Relations

Westen and co-workers have put forward a detailed and well-researched scoring system for interpersonal object relations, that is, for scoring the nature of social interactions described in TAT stories and the ways in which interpersonal relations are internalized.

Westen, Lohr, Silk, Kerber, and Goodrich (1989) have put forward a manual for scoring what they have referred to as Social Cognition and Object Relations (SCORS) on the TAT. The theoretical background for the scales is an interesting combination of social-cognitive, cognitive-developmental, and psychoanalytic approaches. The intent is to measure "the extent to which the subject clearly differentiates the perspectives of self and others; sees the self and others as having stable, enduring multidimensional dispositions; and sees the self and others as psychological beings with complex motives and subjective experience" (Westen et al., p. 29).

In a later development, Westen (1995) differentiated between eight elements: complexity of representation of people; affective quality of representations; emotional investment in relationships; emotional investment in values and moral standards; understanding of social causality; experience and management of aggressive impulses; self-esteem; and identity and coherence of the self.

In a 1995 study, Hibbard, Hilsenroth, Hibbard, and Nash related a Rorschach-based object representation scale and the Westen TAT scales to each other and also to measures of intelligence and psychopathology. In this study, the results were found to support the construct validity of object representations and an affective—but not a cognitive–structural—linkage between object relations and pathology.

Those Westen scales that are more affective in nature (Affect Tone [AT] and Understanding of Social Causality [USC]) have emerged quite favorably from studies relating them to relevant criteria. Thus, Berends, Westen, Leigh, and Silbert (1990) found significant correlations of AT with a measure of social adjustment and ego development. Bernstein and Perry (1995) worked with the original four Object Relations and Social Cognition (ORSC) scales with four diagnostic groups. These investigators found that antisocial subjects had the lowest scores on the two affective scales (AT and Capacity for Emotional Investment and Moral Standards).

Porcerelli, Cogan, and Hibbard (1998) correlated both the cognitive and the affective scales of the ORSC with personality disorder scales from the Millon Clinical Multiaxial Inventory II (Millon, 1987). The cognitive scales did not correlate with the Millon scales, but correlations were found with the affective scales, the largest being with the Millon Antisocial Personality Disorder Scale.

It should be noted that Westen's scoring of object relations has been shown to distinguish between borderline, major depressive, and normal subjects (Westen, Lohr, Silk, Gold, & Kerber, 1990). The system has also been shown to be useful with borderline adolescent subjects (Westen, Ludolph, Block, Wixom, & Wiss, 1991) and with girls who had been sexually abused (Nigg et al., 1991).

In sum, the system developed by Westen shows both good criterion-related validity and good construct validity. It is, however, time consuming, which at this point limits its usefulness for clinical purposes.

Diversity Issues in TAT Use and Alternatives to the TAT

It is highly important to pay attention to individual differences with regard to culture, race, and ethnicity, as well as age, gender, health status, and sexual orientation when using the TAT in psychological testing. As with all psychological tests, the examiner must consider whether the TAT is an appropriate instrument for the intended population, and how interpretation of the results should be influenced by cultural factors. This chapter will discuss the appropriateness of using the TAT with different cultural groups, alternative storytelling tests that have been developed for use with various populations, and issues to consider in interpretation of results.

Retief (1987) provided a very brief review of the history of the cross-cultural use of projective techniques. Hermann Rorschach used his test to study different cultural groups (Rorschach, 1921/1942). In 1935, Bleuler and Bleuler compared the Rorschach responses of European and Moroccan subjects (cited in Butcher & Pancheri, 1976). In a summary of the cross-cultural usage of projective tests, the TAT emerged as the favorite technique (Baran, 1970; cited in Retief, 1987). In 1983, Andor compiled a bibliography of studies and found that 6 of the 32 studies done among African Americans that were listed under "personality assessment" involved adaptations of the TAT, 1 used the original TAT, and 9 used the Rorschach. However, it is noted by Retief that most of these studies did not account for the unfamiliarity of the materials to the subjects in their interpretations and did not take into account the subjects' cultural frame of reference. Therefore, the interpretations likely over-pathologized the subjects.

Today it is widely recognized that cultural issues must be considered in order to maximize validity of test results and avoid mislabeling individuals who are tested. The American Psychological Association's Ethics Code (American Psychological Association, 1992) emphasizes that examiners are obligated to become knowledgeable about and be responsible about test usage and interpretation with regard to individual differences. The following two examples of ethical codes make this responsibility clear:

1.08 Human Differences

Where differences of age, gender, race, ethnicity, national origin, religion, sexual orientation, disability, language, or socioeconomic status significantly affect psychologists' work concerning particular individuals or groups, psychologists obtain the training, experience, consultation, or supervision necessary to ensure the competence of their services, or they make appropriate referrals. (p. 6)

2.04c Use of Assessment in General and with Special Populations

Psychologists attempt to identify situations in which particular interventions or assessment techniques or norms may not be applicable or may require adjustment in administration or interpretation because of factors such as individuals' gender, age, race, ethnicity, national origin, religion, sexual orientation, disability, language, or socioeconomic status. (p. 9)

Retief (1987) defined culture as a system of meanings (a definition originally developed by Max Weber), and stated that psychological tests are examples of meaning systems that are based in the Western cultures of those who developed the tests. He explained, however, that projective tests may be less sensitive to "shifts in meaning" (p. 49) across cultures than more structured tests, because they are more holistic and phenomenologically based. Nevertheless, Retief argues that projective techniques have to be revised and adapted for cross-cultural application in order to exercise some form of control over shifts in meaning and that the validity of tests depends on "good test construction methods, the constructs chosen and the signs and symbols used in the stimulus material" (p. 49).

☐ Alternatives to the TAT

Age Diversity

Early in the history of the TAT, before issues of cross-cultural usage were commonly addressed, it was recognized that different versions of the technique could be useful for different populations, increasing the potential for subjects' identification with the characters. The diversity issue first addressed was diversity in terms of age. Several of the original TAT cards depict children (cards 1, 7GF, 8BM) and several depict older adults (cards 6BM, 7BM). Alternatives were developed to appeal more and elicit more relevant information from individuals belonging to these age groups. More recently, alternative stimuli have been developed for use with different cultural groups.

The CAT and the CAT-H

The idea that it is important for subjects to be able to identify with the characters depicted in TAT pictures is not a new idea. The CAT is a technique created by Bellak and Bellak (1948) as an alternative to the TAT for use with children. The characters used in the pictures are animals, as it was believed that children could identify more readily with animals than with people (Bellak & Abrams, 1997). The CAT cards depict situations likely to elicit stories revealing dynamics central for children, such as feeding issues, sibling rivalry, and relationships with parents.

The CAT is easier to use cross-culturally than the TAT because the animal characters are relatively ambiguous with regard to sex and culture. Some of the furniture and objects, however, are more culturally specific. There are Indian (Chowdhury, 1960a) and Indonesian adaptations of the CAT in which the furniture and some of the animals are changed to be more culturally familiar.

Although there is literature to support the idea that children more readily identify with animals than with people, it has been found that many children do respond better to human character stimuli. Therefore, the CAT-H (Bellak & Bellak, 1965) was developed, a version of the CAT with human figures depicting the same scenes as the CAT animals. For a review of studies comparing the use of animal and human character stimuli, see Bellak and Hurvich (1966); results have been mixed.

The RATC

The RATC (McArthur & Roberts, 1982) is a more recently developed projective storytelling technique for children and adolescents aged 6 to 15. It has several advantages over the CAT, including a standardized scoring system for quantifying adaptive and clinical personality dimensions and more modern pictures. Validity studies have had quite positive findings (Palomares, Crowley, Worchel, Olson, & Rae, 1991).

The SAT and the GAT

Analogous to the development of the CAT for children, the SAT (Bellak & Bellak, 1973) was developed with pictures showing older individuals in situations involving issues encountered by many elderly people, such as illness and loneliness. The SAT cards can be useful in understanding how issues of aging are impacting subjects. With older adults, one may also choose to use the GAT (Wolk & Wolk, 1971). The pictures may be perceived as more positively toned than the SAT.

Cultural Diversity

It has been argued that Murray's TAT cards are not appropriate for use with non-White populations, because some studies have reported that minority groups respond negatively to the TAT (Thompson & Bachrach, 1951). Several studies have shown that subjects react more positively to stimuli showing characters of their own race. Bailey and Green (1977) found that African American subjects rated a set of TAT cards that depicted Black characters more positively than the original TAT cards. African American female college students gave longer stories and scored higher on need for achievement when responding to Black, rather then White, stimulus characters (Cowan & Goldberg, 1967).

Thompson (1949) created a set of picture stimuli substituting Black for White figures, otherwise keeping the stimuli as similar as possible to Murray's TAT cards, and found that the average story length of the adult male African American subjects was significantly greater than in response to the original cards. He interpreted this as evidence that members of minority groups are better able to identify and empathize with characters who are racially congruent with themselves. However, others have criticized this interpretation and have not been able to replicate Thompson's findings (Korchin, Mitchell, & Meltzoff, 1950).

Deplu and Kimbrough (1982) found that African American children responded with more positive themes to the Themes Concerning Blacks (TCB) cards, which show Black figures, than to TAT cards. The children selected mostly TCB cards as the cards they liked best, and were more likely to choose TAT cards as ones they liked less. The TCB responses had mostly a positive feeling-tone, but were not longer than the TAT responses (Triplett & Brunson, 1982). However, it should be noted that because there was no comparison group of White children in either of these studies, it is unknown whether the positive themes and card preferences are due to racial congruence of the subjects and stimuli, or are more simply attributable to something else about the TCB stimuli as compared to the TAT.

Alternative techniques have been developed in response to the argument that Murray's TAT stimuli may not be optimal for use with minority subjects. Whereas Murray's pictures present White characters, the new stimuli typically represent more diverse populations, or populations of the specific culture or race to be assessed using that test, and often are set in situations more familiar to non-White individuals. The main argument for the development of new test stimuli is that subjects respond more readily and more validly when they are maximally able to identify with the stimulus characters and the situational context.

It should be remembered, however, that the assumption that increased similarity between subject and stimulus characters results in increased identification has not been empirically proven. Neither has the assumption that greater identification results in better assessment results. One of the few studies specifically investigating the relationship between similarity of subjects and card characters and degree of projection did not support the utility of increased similarity. TAT stories of 52 college students were scored for projection, defined as amount of fantasy, amount of affect, intensity of affect, and length. No significant increase in projection as a result of matching the sex of subject to the sex of stimulus figures was found (Katz, Russ, & Overholser, 1993). Although gender is a different variable than race or culture, one should not simply assume that similarity between subjects and stimulus characters automatically increases test utility.

It also remains unproven whether more identification with stimulus characters necessarily facilitates the usefulness and validity of the test results. Taken to the extreme, this logic would lead to the suggestion that the best technique would be to ask subjects to create a story with a mirror as a stimulus (Korchin, Mitchell, & Meltzoff, 1950). It could also be argued that if the characters and settings are too familiar, the face validity of the test will elicit more defenses and be less revealing of intrapsychic conflict. However, accepting the assumptions discussed above, alternative stimuli to Murray's TAT have been developed that are intended to be of increased use with a variety of cultural groups. Several of the more promising ones are presented below.

An Indian Modification of the TAT

Chowdhury (1960b) developed TAT stimuli for use with Indian populations. The set is composed of 14 cards: 12 adapted from the original TAT pictures, and 2 additional ones representing themes important to Indian culture not represented in the original TAT, that is, joint family and religious fantasy. The stimuli depict Indian characters wearing traditional Indian apparel in similar situations to the original cards. For example, in card 1 an Indian stringed instrument, a Tanpura, is substituted for a violin. Chowdhury administered the 14 cards to 260 individuals, including Upper Caste Hindus, Lower Caste Hindus, and Muslims. Results indicate that responses were revealing of the subjects' inner drives, wishes, stresses, and anxieties, and the responses were found to be congruent with Rorschach results of the subjects.

TEMAS

TEMAS (Costantino et al., 1981) was developed as a multicultural apperceptive projective technique for use with minority and nonminority children. It is an acronym for "Tell-Me-A-Story" in English, and means "themes" in Spanish. There are two parallel versions, each consisting of 23 cards, including 9-card short forms. The minority version depicts urban ethnic minority figures, cultural themes and symbols, and urban settings; the nonminority version shows predominantly White characters with identical themes and settings. Other differences between the TEMAS and the TAT are that TEMAS has color pictures and the pictures are less ambiguous.

A detailed scoring system was developed for TEMAS. Stories can be scored for 18 Cognitive Functions (such as Reaction Time, Imagination, Event Omissions), 9 Personality Functions (including Aggression, Self-Concept, and Reality Testing), and 7 Affective Functions (e.g., Happy, Fearful, Angry). TEMAS was standardized on 642 Black, White, and Hispanic children from New York City public schools. Interrater reliability for the Personality Functions ranged from 75%–95% in a sample of 20 nonminority protocols (Costantino, Malgady, Casullo, & Castillo, 1991). Internal consistency (for the long form) among cards for specific scoring variables had a median value of .73 for a Hispanic sample and .62 for a Black sample of children.

This test's usefulness has been empirically supported. Costantino et al. (1981) reported that bilingual examiners administered six TAT cards and then six TEMAS cards to 76 Hispanic children aged 9–12. It was found that, on average, children demonstrated greater verbal productivity (greater number of words in the stories) in response to TEMAS than to TAT cards. The effect of the increased productivity was greater for girls than for boys. These results remained after controlling for the effect of verbal ability and rapport and fatigue. Interestingly, children were more likely to respond to TEMAS in Spanish (61%) and were more likely to respond to the TAT in English (43%). Most notably, 18% of the sample used English for the TAT, then switched to Spanish for TEMAS. This is presented as evidence for the Hispanic sample of children's enhanced comfort with the TEMAS, in that they were more at ease using their ethnic language.

Interpretation of the results in the Costantino et al. (1981) study can be questioned on several issues. To what extent is word count a meaningful indicator of the test's worth in a specific population? Does quantity imply quality of response interpretation? It should also be considered that differences other than cultural relevance, such as chromatic pictures and more structured scenes, may have caused the longer responses. Thompson and Bachrach (1951) found that length of response was significantly greater to chromatic cards than to achromatic cards, and that this pattern emerged for White and for Black groups of subjects. This is thought to be a function of increased emotional tone and reality brought by colored pictures. Another limitation of the Costantino et al. (1981) study is the failure to counterbalance order of test administration; perhaps the longer protocols of TEMAS were brought about by that test being administered second, when subjects were "warmed up."

Despite the limitations of this study, the validity of TEMAS has been supported in several ways. TEMAS stories of 210 Puerto Rican children were scored for specific personality functions that significantly predicted the children's scores on ego development, behavior ratings, delay of gratification, self-concept of competence, disruptiveness, and aggression after a course of psychotherapy. TEMAS profiles predicted 6%–22% of the variance in treatment outcome scores, independent of pretest scores (Malgady, Costantino, & Rogler, 1984). TEMAS was also found to accurately discriminate between clinical and nonclinical groups of low SES Hispanic and African American children 89% of the time (Costantino, Malgady, Rogler, & Tsui, 1988).

APT

The Apperceptive Personality Test (APT; Holmstrom, Silber, & Karp, 1990) is a relatively new projective story technique that was developed for use with adolescent and adult subjects of any racial background. The APT is comprised of an eight-card set that is administered to all subjects, in contrast to the TAT and other techniques in which the examiner chooses which cards are to be used. The benefits of having a constant set of cards administered are that test results are more easily compared with each other, research is facilitated, and examiner bias is reduced. An effort was made to create male and female APT characters of differing ages and ethnicities. They are depicted in common, modern settings involving a range of potential social and interpersonal themes.

A strong advantage of the APT is that it includes a single standard scoring procedure. First, the eight cards are administered, with subjects writing down their stories. Following this administration, subjects refer to their stories while completing the APT questionnaire, which asks subjects to answer six questions about each story. The questions ask about the relationships between characters, feelings and actions of the characters, who the hero is, the outcome of the story and adjectives describing the characters. The information is coded by subjects from their own stories, thus there is no interpretation on the part of the examiner (of course, traditional interpretation can also be done with the stories as well). Responses are then compared to norms.

Overall, mean test-retest reliability for APT scores was found to be .75. Evidence supporting the validity of the APT includes relationships between APT responses and MMPI results, such as significant correlations between APT indices of hostility and psychopathology and hostility on the MMPI, and the MMPI depression scale and the APT score for unhappiness (Holmstrom et al., 1990). When compared with the TAT, the APT stories showed less aggression and less achievement imagery, but not significantly different story outcome ratings. To summarize, the APT stimuli are more representative and contemporary than those of many other apperceptive techniques, and can be used in the traditional manner as well as with a reasonably psychometrically sound scoring system. These preliminary results are encouraging.

Draw-A-Person as Stimulus

French (1993) proposed an alternate storytelling technique for use with minority children. It combines Draw-A-Person with the TAT, avoiding potential biases in test stimuli. The child subject is asked to draw a picture of him- or herself. At a second session, the child is presented with the picture, and asked to tell the examiner something about the person in the drawing. Then the child is asked to "Draw a picture of you and your family," and questions are asked following the TAT format: "Tell me a story about this family. What is happening in the story? Who is the hero? What are the people thinking and feeling? What is the outcome of the story?" French uses this technique with Hispanic, Mexican, and American Indian children in the Southwest and states that this approach minimizes discomfort to the child and requires less interpretation by the examiner, limiting the opportunity for misinterpretation. However, the high face validity of the technique may increase the impact of social desirability on responses.

Development of Alternative Stimuli

The influence of the test stimuli should not be underestimated. When story responses to the *Family of Man* photo essay collection, published by the Museum of Modern Art, were compared with responses to Murray's TAT pictures, it was found that the *Family of Man* pictures yielded responses balanced between positive- and negative-toned stories, and higher energy stories; whereas the TAT yielded more negatively toned stories, and lower energy stories (Ritzler et al., 1980). This study demonstrates the importance of the role of stimuli used in projective techniques, underscores the importance of conscientious test development, and reminds examiners to consider the realistic aspects of the stimuli perception during interpretation.

The common theme in the development of new stimuli for storytelling assessment techniques is that the characters and the contexts should be relevant to the subjects. For this reason, it could be argued that there should be different sets of stimuli for different populations. If stimuli are tailored to particular racial or cultural groups, great care should be taken to avoid prejudicial intentions and building harmful stereotypes into the pictures. For example, the TAT-Z (Erasmus, 1975), an early adaptation of the TAT for use with African Americans, is criticized by Retief (1987) because it was intended to measure attitudes toward White authority. The cards depict situations that would likely provoke angry feelings in most minority subjects. Interpretation of the resulting stories could easily be biased.

Retief (1987) suggested that new tests should be developed with more structured stimuli, designed to assess specific areas of personality makeup, such as aggression and need for achievement. Constructs should be chosen that have meaning across different cultures and can be operationalized in terms of observable behavior. Retief argued that tests that select focus on specific areas, rather than include as many areas for interpretation as possible will minimize errors in interpretation. Formal scoring systems could also reduce misinterpretation.

Sherwood (1957) offered detailed, specific guidelines for designing a set of TAT cards for cross-cultural use. First, he has several suggestions to maximize the usefulness of the pictures as projective stimuli:

1. The pictorial images should strike a balance between being realistic enough to allow subjects to identify with some of the content and being vague enough to allow for a variety of interpretations of the content.

2. The pictures should be left somewhat incomplete, so that imagination is required of subjects in their associations.

3. Stimuli should be densely packed into each picture, to allow associations to a wide range of relationships, values, attitudes, and themes, and to have a greater possibility of corresponding to the unconscious content of the subjects.

This last suggestion, to densely compress stimuli into the pictures, is contrary to Retief's (1987) recommendation that pictures should be more selective and focused to reduce errors in interpretation. Less structure would make interpretation more difficult, but increase the projective nature of the task.

Sherwood (1957) suggested that the set of cards as a whole should be varied. He believed that contrast in the visual impact of the stimuli helps engage subjects and holds their interest throughout the assessment. Additionally, variety helps the examiner obtain more representative information about subjects and offers the opportunity to learn about the subject's reactions to different situations. For example, the pictures should vary in terms of emotional tone: some should be positively toned, some negatively toned, and some should be more neutral. A criticism of Murray's TAT is that the majority of the cards are negatively toned. A variety of basic family relationships should be represented, including subject-mother, subject-father, and subject-siblings. Other important relationships should be depicted as well, such as same-sex and opposite-sex peer relationships. It is also useful to show relationships that are less conventional and less familiar, to elicit more fantasy material. A range in the number of characters shown in different cards is helpful in determining the subject's ability to integrate objects.

Finally, Sherwood (1957) offered suggestions for stimuli development that are specific to cross-cultural use. It is believed that projection will be maximally effective if subjects feel comfortable and can identify with the characters in the cards. Therefore, it is recommended that the human figures represented in the stimuli are recognizable as belonging to the subject's own cultural group. This includes appropriate physical traits, clothing, hairstyles, and gestures. It may also be desirable to include some characters outside the subject's immediate culture group who are a significant part of the larger society in which the subject's group is embedded. Physical environments that are familiar to the subjects and implied interpersonal relationships that are patterned after relationships commonly found in the culture are also important in creating pictures that are culturally appropriate.

It is proposed that the effectiveness of the pictures as appropriate projective stimuli can be evaluated by looking at the length of elicited responses; the relevance of responses to the content areas the pictures are intended to tap; and the degree of fantasy the pictures generate, measured by the number of introduced material, varieties of responses in plot, and the imaginative, creative quality of the responses (Sherwood, 1957).

It should be mentioned that despite the soundness of Sherwood's (1957) recommendations, unfortunately there seems to have been minimal application of his principles. His paper has only been rarely cited (Dana, 1999).

☐ Which Test to Use?

The question arises as to whether one should choose to use Murray's TAT or to use one of the alternative techniques, and if so, which one? The clearest advantages of using the original TAT is the examiner's prior experience with the technique, and the wealth of published data on the technique. Norms published by Eron (1950, 1953) provide examiners with information with which to compare subjects' responses. Examiners' own experiences, following many TAT administrations, also afford much data about the conventionality or originality of responses. This sum of information is highly valuable, because valid TAT interpretation relies on interpreting that which is uniquely reflective of the individual being assessed. For example, if the majority of subjects attribute violent behavior to a character stimulus, one would be less likely to interpret such a response as meaning something about an individual subject. In order to recognize popular and original TAT responses, an ongoing accumulation of knowledge about the assessment technique is needed. On the other hand, exploring promising new techniques is the only way to accumulate a knowledge base about them. Research must clearly be done for appropriate population norms before the newer tests can be used with any confidence.

Whenever a test is selected for use, the body of research evaluating the test's validity should be considered. Another less formal way to evaluate the uses of a test is to use Sherwood's (1957) criteria, as discussed in the previous section, on a sample of subjects, looking in depth at the qualitative and quantitative features of responses by the subjects.

☐ Considering Individual Differences in Assessment

The issue of individual differences must be considered, regardless of which storytelling technique is used. There are some general considerations that should be kept in mind in all kinds of testing, but perhaps particularly when using less structured techniques, and when assessing persons of different cultures than the test's creators or the populations on which the test was normed. Although this chapter has focused on differences in culture and race as important factors, individuals, of course, also differ in economic status, religion, sexual orientation, gender, health status, and so on. It is most important that an examiner remembers that he or she is testing an individual who has been influenced in many ways by the environment because of his or her membership in various subgroups of society. Carefully considering how such memberships may affect responses to assessment, in addition to trying to understand how personality or psychopathology contributes, is essential to valid interpretation of results.

A suggested structure for formulating the relevance of cultural issues to diagnosis is presented in Appendix I in the DSM-IV (4th ed.; American Psychiatric Association, 1994). It is suggested that the cultural identity of the individual and the degree of involvement in the original and host cultures be considered. The culture's explanation or perceived cause for an individual's behavioral or affective disturbance should also be determined. The examiner should also note how the individual's culture relates to the psychosocial environment and level of functioning—for example, social and instrumental supports. The DSM-IV includes a glossary of commonly encountered culturally linked diagnoses. That the DSM-IV devotes an appendix to the issue of culture should impress upon the reader the current emphasis on addressing the issue of culture in diagnosis.

Maximally understanding the person's background will reduce the risk of overpathologizing. The ethical standards requiring psychologists to obtain appropriate training, experience, consultation, or supervision in how individual differences impact testing or to make appropriate referrals is intended to address this point. Ethical standards also require psychologists to carefully consider the appropriateness of norms for the individual being tested. Examiners should always ask themselves: How similar is the individual to the population on which the norms are based? How might the differences between the individual and the norm population impact interpretation of the individual's responses? This is true not only in cases where formal norms are used, but also when the population to which the individual is being compared is the total of previous subjects the particular examiner has tested. Finally, variables that are scored should be of importance to the culture of the individual being tested, preferably derived from the structure and content of stories from a particular culture, rather than automatically coming from Anglo-American sources (Dana, 1999).

Using culturally sensitive or culturally appropriate tests is not a sufficient alternative to a culturally sensitive, knowledgeable examiner. Administering the test with social etiquette appropriate to the subject's culture is recommended (Dana, 1996) and may facilitate rapport and valid results. Relevant aspects of etiquette may include appropriate greetings, eye contact, and body language. To further avoid overpathologizing, it is recommended that details of the circumstances under which the test was given be recorded and addressed, including instructions given and interactions between the subject and the examiner. The influence of language and translation problems should also be determined. In general, one would rather "err on the side of health" when interpreting test responses rather than overpathologizing or mislabeling a subject. Always consider possible alternative explanations for unusual responses. Cultural differences should be considered as a salient alternative explanation.

The TAT in Psychotherapy

The TAT has a long association with the psychotherapeutic endeavor. Combs (1946) wrote of the abundance of autobiographical material that is typically contained in TAT stories, thus providing the therapist with important background information about test subjects. In a later study, Hoffman and Kuperman (1990) noted how discussion of repetitive TAT themes in psychotherapy may help in singling out a history of trauma.

Ullmann (1957) found significant correlations between TAT scores of psychiatric patients on the one hand, and hospital status and group therapy scale predictions on the other. In a 1960 study, Fairweather et al. used the TAT to assess the effectiveness of psychotherapy modalities. These authors found a significant interaction effect in that group therapy and control groups showed more positive TAT change for nonpsychotic than for psychotic psychiatric subjects while individual therapy produced more positive TAT change for long-term psychotic individuals.

The TAT has also been used fairly extensively in outcome studies in connection with psychotherapy research (e.g., Coche & Sillitti, 1983; Dymond, 1954; Frank & Gunderson, 1990; Goldman & Greenblatt, 1955).

One line of investigation with relevance to psychotherapy is the study of what the TAT may assess in terms of the "levels" or depth of personality reached by different measures. Thus, Stone and Dellis (1960) found that the TAT reached lower levels than an intelligence test and a sentence completion test, but not as low as the Rorschach or the Draw-A-Person

Test. In a somewhat related study, Theiner (1962) found more acceptable needs expressed on an incomplete sentence test, with less acceptable needs expressed on the TAT (the less structured measure).

The TAT has also been suggested as a useful adjunct in marital therapy (Araoz, 1972), as useful in selecting people for group psychotherapy (Ullmann, 1957), and also as effective in quickly clarifying psychodynamic issues in very brief psychotherapy (Bellak, Abrams, & Ackermann-Engel, 1992). This latter use of the TAT is certainly quite relevant to the present time- and cost-conscious mental health climate. Holzberg (1963) suggested using the TAT to allow patients to practice "adaptive regression" in a safe and controlled situation. Aronow et al. (1994) have used a Consensus TAT in conjunction with the Consensus Rorschach to help clarify couple dynamics. It might be useful to recall that Morgan and Murray (1935), when first promulgating the TAT, recommended its use in connection with brief psychotherapy.

Hoffman and Kuperman (1990), in a rather creative study, presented a situation in which two co-therapists wrote their own TAT stories to the same cards used by a 13-year-old male subject. One of the therapists emphasized maladaptive qualities of the boy's stories while the other therapist emphasized healthy aspects of the stories. A joint discussion with the subject was then held in which the boy was found to gravitate to the healthier aspects. The TAT was thus used in this creative fashion as an actual therapeutic tool. This echoes a very early suggestion by Rosenzweig (1948) in which the subject could be encouraged to make his or her own interpretations of TAT stories.

In our experience (expressed elsewhere, Aronow et al., 1994) projective techniques can serve four principal functions in the psychotherapeutic endeavor:

1. A road map of dynamics, conflicts, ego strengths and weaknesses, social aspects of functioning, and so on prior to the onset of therapy. This is, of course, the more traditional use to which the TAT and other projective techniques have been put in connection with psychotherapy.

2. An assessment of progress, either during the course of therapy or at the very end. The latter can be particularly useful if there is a "before" measure to provide contrast.

3. A technique to clarify blockages that may occur in the course of psychotherapy that might otherwise be impenetrable.

4. An actual tool that can be used for insight and change in psychotherapy

that occurs when the therapist shares the interpretation of responses with the subject. This last use of projective techniques is, of course, the most demanding in terms of clinical skill and timing.

The first use of the TAT and other projective techniques is far from new. We have tried to summarize such use of the technique, particularly in chapters 3, 5, and 6. The second use of the TAT is exemplified in particular in protocol # 1, presented in this chapter. The subject was a college student who was administered the TAT and other projective and nonprojective techniques both before and after a course of psychotherapy. The contrasts seen in the TAT stories are instructive in terms of the changes that occurred in the subject in the interim.

The third use noted—involving the identification of blockages in psychotherapy and the subsequent breakdown of the blockages—is presented in protocol # 2 in this chapter. We wrote of a similar use of the Rorschach in such a context in our former volume (Aronow et al., 1994). It has been our experience that this third use of projective techniques often merges with the fourth since it is the sharing of projective interpretations that typically breaks the logjams.

The latter two uses of the TAT and other projective techniques, represent something of a departure from the traditional view of such techniques as "tests." Nonetheless, the blurring of boundaries between the evaluation and the therapeutic process has a long history and has recently become a much more mainstream view in psychology.

The view of evaluation as having the ability to merge with and contribute to the psychotherapy process can be said to date back at least to the writings of Jung (1961), who wrote about the treatment of a schizophrenic woman in the early 1900s. He indicated that the woman was given feedback about association test performance and then quickly improved to the point where she was able to be discharged from the hospital. Jung felt that the assessment process enabled the woman to tell her "secret story," which thus began the psychotherapeutic process for her. Jung thus noted that it is difficult to discern exactly where the assessment process ends and the psychotherapy process begins.

In a 1960 article, Harrower suggested discussing some of the patients' projective test responses with them, a procedure she called "projective counseling." This was clearly a break from the more traditional approach as exemplified by Klopfer and Kelley (1946), who warned of the potential damage that can be done by the sharing of projective interpretations with clients.

Over the years a number of other authors reported on the positive consequences of the sharing of clinical information and projective and other test data and interpretations with patients. These studies have included the works of Appelbaum (1990); Aronow and Reznikoff (1971); Craddick (1972, 1975); Fischer (1970, 1972); Gass and Brown (1992); Roth, Wolford, and Meisel (1980); and Stein, Furedy, Simonton, and Neuffer (1979).

Finn and Tonsager (1992) published a rather unique study in this respect in that it constituted a strictly empirical study of the effects of MMPI test feedback. These authors based their feedback on their own "collaborative model" of the process they developed. It was found in this study that subjects given feedback reported a significant decrease in stress and an increase in self-esteem. Interestingly, these positive effects of the feedback were found to have increased two weeks after the feedback was rendered.

☐ Protocol # 1

The following are before and after psychotherapy TAT protocols from a 19-year-old college freshman, which two of the current authors had previously published (Aronow & Reznikoff, 1971).

The client had presented at the university counseling center with symptoms of radical personality change, alienation from people, and growing feelings of unreality. The client came from a large family in which both parents were alcoholics, with the father quite verbally and physically abusive toward him. He was tested at the onset of therapy, and again after seven months of once-per-week psychotherapy with the first author. Only selected TAT stories are presented.

First Testing

Card 3BM

When the police arrived they had to arrest the poor soul. He was to be tried for suicide. The D.A. was running for governor and needed a conviction so they were going to hold this guy for murder in the first degree. The scene was in the courtroom: "They've just put the corpse on the stand. He refused to talk and didn't request an attorney. He's been on a hunger strike, but you bleeding hearts better not feel sorry for him. He's a murderer. We knew that he was planning to kill himself for some time now. So it was contemplated and premeditated. (Pointing to the body) "Deny that! I dare you! Silence proves your guilt." The D.A. smiles at the jury: "Sure, he was depressed, but it's our right to be depressed. Would any of you have denied George Washington at Valley Forge his right to be depressed? Of course not! Did he shoot himself? No. Can we let this murderous villain go out of here a free corpse to corrupt our soil? No." It was all very effective and the jury brought in the verdict of "Guilty." The man was sentenced to life in the state pen, but they let him go for good behavior.

Summary: A man who committed suicide is tried for murder and convicted.

Card 8BM

The little prince of Estonia stood by watching the doctors operate to save the life of a royal guardsman. "Certainly screams a lot, doesn't he?" the boy said. "He's not made of tough stuff, I guess." The doctor, having listened to this for the last hour, gripped the knife. He thought to himself: "Let's have a look to see what you're made of, fresh punk." Then he sighed and continued his work. The man holding the light was sharing in the thoughts of the doctor. He too was a guard and knew it could easily have been him on the table. Being a guard to this cruel and unpopular prince was no easy task. The man on the table asked the doctor: "My chances, my chances . . . " "Poor," came the slow reply. The little prince sneered: "You don't deserve to speak, I almost was killed because of you." The dying guard mustered his last strength and rose from the table. "Give me that knife, doctor." "What are you going to do?" Before the answer came, the prince lay dead.

Summary: A dying guardsman murders an insensitive prince.

Card 9BM

In a depression, few men have jobs and these fellows are no exception. Their spirit to work had been robbed, so they returned to nature. They left their homes and families in search of something. Who knows? They would find it down the road. They quickly spent their "fortunes" and found themselves hungry. Five hungry men can be a problem. They knew they had to eat or starve to death. They finally arrived at a solution and if you look at how many men there are in the picture you'll know. Snake eyes don't always come up, but they sure did this time.

Summary: Hungry men during a depression eat one of their fellows.

Card 13MF

He knew she loved him. For over a year they had been planning to get married. They had never slept together before, but this time they would.

As he lay there in bed with her, she said: "I love you." And he knew it was true. He thought for a long moment. He turned to her and slowly he choked her. As she died she said, "I love you." "I know, and you always will." He called the police and now stands over his love. He had her love now and could never lose it. ("Kind of maudlin.")

Summary: Lovers have sex for the first time, and he murders her so he can never lose her love.

Second Testing

Card 3BM

Toy guns, all in fun, the poor boy shot himself. His head lies on the bed, his mother bore him to the bed. For his twelfth birthday, he wanted a gun. His mother bought him one, it wasn't real. "I wish this was a real gun," he'd often say. One day, he got his wish and shot himself. Moral: Don't wish too hard for what you want, you might get it.

Summary: A boy wishes for a gun, gets it, and is shot by it.

Card 8BM

"This barn wasn't always an operating room," the boy whispered. "Once there were cows and horses in here. Do you remember, father?" The boy's father lies on the table. Moments ago he had been shot accidentally while hunting. Doctor Schreider, a veterinarian, was fortunately next door and had come to help. Now it looked bad. The boy bit his lip nervously. "Father will live, won't he? I'm sure the cows don't mind the noise." His father died just then. "I saw an old hoot owl in here. We'll have to chase him out, he's frightening the calves." The doctor tried to tell the boy, "Son, your father is dead." The boy winced for a moment, just a fleeting second, and continued, "I don't think we'll have rats again this year, do you, father?" (I was kind to him this time.)

Summary: A father dies in surgery by a veterinarian after an accident.

Card 9BM

He had just come upon the scene. Three bodies lay in the clearing. He took out his pad. "That makes seven, eight and nine. Nine more we've found today." He had an easy job as Official Calculator of Corpi (plural of corpses) for the Union of Friendly States. He enjoyed following the army to count the dead, somehow it reminded him of goldfish in a bowl. He went on aways. Suddenly he smelled the familiar gas. "Over here," someone yelled. He became dizzy and collapsed. An official walked up to him. "And that makes 10."

Summary: A "body counter" in a war becomes one of the casualties.

Card 13MF

The smell of gas overwhelmed him as he opened the door. There on the bed lay the girl that he would have married. "Why?" This was the plaguing question. We homo sapiens secretly rejoice in our guilt and flatter ourselves as the cause of catastrophe. Openly we pound our chests and cry "Mea culpa" while we marvel at our strength. He was no different. A gleam came to his eye as he thought of the reputation he had earned. ("Women kill themselves over Ron.") There lay the note. He opened it. "Dearest, I couldn't go on living this lie. Forgive me, John." His face flushed at this humiliation. "Lousy bitch," he murmured, and stormed out.

Summary: A man feels proud of his fiancee's suicide, but then learns he was betrayed.

Interpretation

In the first testing (before therapy) a number of themes are apparent. First, there is a grandiose and removed-from-reality quality to some of the stories (card 3BM, card 8BM). Further, there appears to be a strong conflict with and hostility toward male authority (same cards). It is also unclear with whom the client identifies in the story to 8BM, not a healthy sign. Also on card 8BM, there is grandiosity ("a prince") and the feelings of low self-worth the grandiosity covers up (prince of what was then a non-existent country). The stories to all the cards are creative, but bizarre. Finishing it off, the story to card 13MF demonstrates an almost total lack of trust or ability to handle intimate relationships.

In the second testing (after seven months of psychotherapy) unhealthy trends are still present. Thus, all stories still have an unhappy resolution. The story to card 9BM is still somewhat bizarre (though perhaps not so bad as cannibalism). There is still anger at male authority (card 8BM—father being treated by veterinarian, father's death, comment of "I don't think we'll have rats again" after father's death).

Some improvements, though, are worth noting. As just mentioned, the stories have a less extreme and less bizarre quality. In addition, some tenderness toward a father figure is expressed (card 8BM). Perhaps most important, story themes are less distanced from reality and grandiose, now involving dramas between parents and a son (card 3BM, card 8BM).

The client's clinical picture is consistent with the TAT changes, involving improvement in symptomatology but a continued need for psychotherapy.

☐ Protocol # 2

The following is a Consensus TAT record of a professional couple in their thirties, Mr. and Mrs. M., who were being seen in marriage counseling. The presenting problems involved a difficulty in his being able to communicate feelings, "paralysis" in his career, and her subtle derogation of him, as well as the primary presenting problem—his unwillingness to have children and her insistence on it (which in a way also might be conceptualized as a paralysis on his part). He had kept putting her off on the issue of having children for financial and other practical reasons, but now she refused to wait any longer. Mr. M. also experienced a loss of interest in sex, which may have been related to the issue of having children.

Five cards of the TAT were consensus-administered to the subjects because of the therapist's sense that the counseling of three months duration had become bogged down and that there was some logjam in the counseling, the nature of which was not readily apparent. Cards 1, 3BM, 4, 6BM, and 7BM were consensus-administered to the couple—that is, the TAT was only administered to them together in a session, without individual administrations preceding it. We have noted elsewhere that administering consensus projective techniques in this fashion is quite practical and time-effective (Aronow et al., 1994).

Card 1

Mr. M.: It looks like the boy is trying to decide whether he wants to play the violin.

Mrs. M.: His parents probably told him to practice, but he wants to go out to play with his friends. I think he'll decide to practice.

Mr. M.: Yeah—he decides to play the violin, but he's not happy.

Card 3BM

Mrs. M.: It looks as though someone is very depressed. Is that a knife on the floor?

Mr. M.: It looks like a guy who doesn't know what to do. Should he kill himself? He's torn. Maybe his girlfriend just broke up with him.

Mrs. M.: I think that this person, with time, recovers. Nothing drastic happens—it will all end up okay.

Mr. M.: I'll go with that story.

Card 4

Mrs. M.: It looks like he's turning away—he doesn't want to talk to her. Maybe he's having an affair and she wants to confront him. They're both angry.

Mr. M.: I don't see that. I think that something is bothering him and he just wants to be left alone.

Mrs. M.: Maybe we could just say that she has something she wants to talk to him about and he doesn't want to listen.

Mr. M.: Yeah, I could go with that.

Card 6BM

Mr. M.: It's a guy and his mother—he just told her some bad news. Maybe the father just had a heart attack and died. They both look very sad.

Mrs. M.: They both look stunned. There's a lot to be said, and stuff to be done—but right now they're both paralyzed. But they'll get over it with the passage of time.

Mr. M.: Sounds okay to me.

Card 7BM

Mrs. M.: It looks like a father trying to talk to his son—give advice—the son is listening.

Mr. M.: (After a long pause). I don't see that. It looks more like the older guy is just selfish and this kid is going to suffer. He hates him. He just wants him to go away.

Mrs. M.: I see it differently—they look like a father and son talking.

Mr. M.: Well, I do. (Mr. M. seems agitated and they do not reach consensus.)

Interpretation

Certain themes are evident in this TAT protocol. First, Mrs. M. seems most interested in their reaching a consensus and in stories reaching a "happy" resolution. Her desire to reach consensus with the husband is most evident on card 4, and she even seeks to do so on card 7BM, though here without success. Other themes evident include Mr. M.'s unhappiness (card 1, card 4, card 7BM), the wife's expression of the current paralysis in the relationship (card 3BM), Mrs. M.'s desire to communicate and the husband's reluctance to do so. Overall, an interesting record, but nothing really new.

Following this session, however, the husband requested an individual session. In this session, he revealed something that he had not spoken of when his individual history was taken—namely, that as a little boy he had been sexually abused on two occasions by two different men. He had never spoken of this to anyone. In subsequent individual sessions, he was able to relate this to doubts about his masculine identity, distrust of others, and after some time he also spoke of a fear that because this had happened to him he might in turn sexually abuse his own children. While these issues might have come out later in the therapy, the TAT procedure clearly facilitated the broaching of this major area without which the counseling likely would have stalled and would have ended unsuccessfully. Individual psychotherapy for the husband was then added as an adjunct to the marital sessions with faster progress then being made.

Integrating the TAT into a Test Report

This chapter will summarize how the information obtained through the TAT can, along with material from other psychological tests, be organized and written into an effective test report. First, an example of an outline of a report will be described, along with potential sources of information for each section of the report. Then, recommendations for enhancing the effectiveness and readability of reports will be discussed. The chapter ends with a brief discussion of computer-generated reports.

Writing a psychological report is a difficult task. It requires the examiner to make sense of a great deal of information (some of which may seem contradictory), find a way to coherently organize the data, summarize the important points, and communicate the results. A good report is one that helps the reader get a feel for what it is like to be with the subject and how the subject experiences the world. This is a complex task, as human experience and interaction is obviously no simple matter.

Developing a strategy for organizing the material to be written up is of great assistance to the writer. The following is an example of an outline with which to systematically arrange the material into an effective report. This outline includes a tremendous amount of information, not all of which needs to be addressed in any one test report. On the other hand, there may be other fruitful topics to include in psychological reports that are not covered here. This sample outline is intended as an example only. The style of the report and the information to be included will undoubtedly vary by the setting in which it is written and by the purpose for which it will be used.

☐ Outline of a Psychological Report

I. Demographic Data

In a heading, include the name of subject, name of examiner, date(s) of examination, date of birth.

II. Tests Administered

List all the tests administered in the current assessment battery. If applicable, cite the reference of the scoring system(s) employed.

III. Referral Question and Brief Background Information

State who referred the subject for evaluation, and the reason for referral. Often directly quoting the referral source or the question to be answered is most effective. Also include, without going into extensive detail, a statement regarding the subject's education, occupation, marital status, medications and dosages, treatment history, past traumatic events, and any other special circumstances that warrant further exploration and may impact on test interpretation.

IV. Behavioral Observations

The examiner should summarize his or her clinical observations of the subject's behavior during assessment. Was there anything unusual or striking about the subject's appearance? To what extent was the subject cooperative and attentive? Was his or her behavior variable? What affects were expressed? What was the subject's attitude toward the test materials and the examiner? Was anything noteworthy regarding the subject's body language?

This section helps the subject of the report "come to life" for the reader, as well as providing a context for interpretation of test material. Generally, this section should focus on demeanor, verbalizations outside of formal test responses, and general behavior. Interpretation of these observations should be made in conjunction with test results in the next section.

V. Interpretation of Test Findings

This is the main section of the report. Here the writer will present the results of the psychological assessment and attempt to flesh out hypotheses about their meaning. The interpretation section is best organized by areas of the subject's functioning, as opposed to being organized by test. For example, all information pertaining to the subject's achievement motivation should be presented together, combining findings from the various tests given. This adds to the presentation of a meaningful, coherent picture of the subject. The writer is encouraged to integrate material from different tests and make conclusions about each area of functioning. Another significant advantage of this type of organization is that it emphasizes the point that the report is about a person, not about assessment instruments. The report should focus on the individual tested, rather than the test material. When mentioned, the test material should only be used as supporting evidence. For example, it is more effective to state, "Mr. D. appears to have angry feelings, as reflected in the arguments in his TAT stories," than, "the TAT stories included many arguments, showing a lot of anger." The former is person-focused, the latter test-focused.

The number of areas one could potentially discuss in this part of the report is infinite. The following provide examples of several areas to address; however, the referral question should ideally determine what needs to be included and what is emphasized in any psychological report.

A. Intellect/Cognitive Functioning

What is the examiner's best estimate of the subject's ability level? If formal cognitive assessment was performed, results should be presented here. A profile of strengths and weaknesses should be described, if available. If no tests with normative comparisons were administered, intelligence can be roughly estimated as below average, average range, or above average based on vocabulary used during assessment and educational attainment.

What is the subject's level of ambition or aspiration? Information regarding this area can often be obtained, for example, by looking at responses to TAT cards 1 and 2, the percentage of whole responses on the Rorschach, emphasis on heads on figure drawings, and observations of the subject's diligence in working on the assessment tasks in general. The degree of consistency among the subject's apparent intelligence, ambition level, and occupation may be noteworthy.

In this section, the examiner may also comment on the subject's cognitive style, or strategy for approaching tasks. This is primarily revealed by the process by which the subject creates the stories, rather than the content. For example, are the stories logical? Are they particularly concrete or abstract? Are they well organized or haphazard? Does the subject focus on details or the total picture? Information regarding cognitive style should be integrated with evidence from other tests, such as the locations used most often on the Rorschach, planning ability on the Bender Visual-Motor Gestalt Test, and style of attempting tasks on formal intelligence tests.

B. Affect

The predominant affects experienced and expressed by the subject should be described. For example, does the subject seem sad, bored, content, pensive? Where does the subject lie on the continuum between emotionally labile and affectively flat? Sources of information regarding the subject's affect can be obtained from the examiner's clinical observations and from projective material. On the TAT stories, the examiner should look at the emotions most frequently demonstrated by the TAT characters, and possibly what triggers various affective responses. The appropriateness of the affects to the situations being described should be considered. Degree of emotional reactivity can be seen by response to potentially more stimulating TAT cards, such as 13BM. The examiner may also consider facial expression on figure drawings, use of color on the Rorschach, and score on Scale 2 of the MMPI-2, which is associated with depression.

C. Self-Regard

How the subject feels about him- or herself is an area that has ramifications for diagnosis and treatment planning. Looking at how the central characters in the TAT stories are depicted will often allow the examiner to make a statement about the subject's self-esteem and degree of self-criticism. For example, are the characters competent? How do they react to making mistakes? Do things work out for them? How do other characters view them? To corroborate this information the examiner can, for example, also look to the size and placement of figure drawings and, perhaps most importantly, the subject's comments about his or her performance during testing.

D. Object Relationships

The richest information provided by the TAT regards to the subject's relationships with others. Information from the TAT may be supplemented with the examiner's observations of the subject's relatedness during testing and attitude toward the examiner as an example of an authority figure. Relationships with different types of figures, such as peers and parents, and attitudes toward those relationships should be described.

For example, the subject's relationship with the mother can be inferred by interpreting responses to older female figures on the TAT, such as in cards 2, 5, 6BM, and 7GF. Responses to cards that depict older males, such as 6GF and 7BM, can reveal something about the subject's relationship with the father. Interpretations can be checked against Sentence Completion Test responses tapping feelings toward mother and father, and possibly by responses to what has been labeled the mother card (card VII) and the father card (card IV) on the Rorschach.

Patterns and perceptions of relationships with peers of the same and opposite sex should be commented on (cards 9BM, 9GF, 4, and 13MF, respectively). Does the subject seem to be active or passive with others? Do the subject's social skills seem adequate? What are the dominant attitudes toward relationships in general? Are they desired or avoided? Are they seen as having positive or negative effects on the subject? What degree of dependency in relationships is expressed? Are difficulties resolved by others or the self? What are the reactions toward relationships ending? What are the topics of the conflicts? How important are relationships to the subject?

Degree of introversion or extroversion and comfort in social situations can also be evaluated by looking at the subject's score on Scale 0 (Social Introversion) of the MMPI-2, while Scale 6 (Paranoia) can provide some insight into the subject's trust in interpersonal relationships (Butcher, 1990).

E. Diagnostic Aspects

In this section, the examiner should summarize information about the subject that has diagnostic implications. Information should be integrated from various tests and several sources of information. What are the areas of the subject's conflicts and anxieties? What are the primary defenses or coping mechanisms used to deal with anxieties and conflicts and how successful are these strategies? A statement may be made about the subject's ties to reality, based on how realistic the stories are and how accurately the visual stimuli are perceived.

Additional evidence from the Rorschach is very helpful here. What is the subject's degree of control over his or her impulses? What is the subject's level of maturity? How much insight does the subject have into his or her own personality and conflicts? MMPI-2 scores on Scales 1 (Hypochondriasis), 2 (Depression), 3 (Hysteria), 4 (Psychopathic Deviate), 6 (Paranoia), 7 (Psychasthenia), and 8 (Schizophrenia) are also valuable sources of corroborative evidence, particularly when interpreted as a profile (see Butcher, 1990, for an introduction to profile interpretation).

Even more than in other areas of the psychological report, one should take great care in the diagnostic section not to make statements that go beyond the purposes of the tests used or exceed the information obtained from the data. All diagnostic information should be backed up by other sources of data including other tests, behavior observations, and background information, and should be consistent with the subject's day-to-day level of functioning.

Depending on the referral question and the setting in which the report is written, the examiner may choose to offer a diagnostic impression or outline a differential diagnosis. For example, this may be more appropriate in a hospital setting, where the psychological assessment will be directly used in treatment planning, than in a school setting, where confidentiality of the report will likely be somewhat limited.

F. Strengths

Every psychological report should speak to the subject's strengths. The examiner should incorporate positive aspects of test findings throughout the report, but may also choose to briefly summarize such capacities at the completion of the interpretation section. This helps to temper the commonplace and unfortunate tendency to pathologize the subject. Examples of strengths to highlight here include intelligence level, aspiration level, level of control over impulses, personality characteristics, insight, and ties to reality. The examiner can also identify circumstances under which the subject's functioning seems to be maximized. Clarifying the subject's strengths is generally helpful in treatment planning.

VI. Summary

A brief summary of the main points of the psychological assessment findings should appear at the end of the report. As in the interpretation section, the summary should focus on the individual tested, not the tests themselves. New material should clearly not be introduced at this point; only information disclosed earlier should be included. In the summary, the referral question, index scores from standardized tests, and the most salient psychodynamic findings should be restated. The writer should keep in mind that this may be the only section read by a busy professional; therefore, it should outline all of the most important points and offer a balanced view of the subject.

VII. Recommendations

The examiner should carefully consider the test findings and offer recommendations regarding the referral question. Additionally, the examiner may suggest further assessment of problem areas. Implications for treatment planning can be offered, including what type of therapy may be most appropriate for the subject, or how the subject's individual strengths can be used to work on his or her areas of weakness. Specific, practical suggestions are most valuable.

☐ Additional Suggestions for Effective Report Writing

The following are suggestions that will enhance the effectiveness of the psychological report. They primarily reflect general issues to keep in mind throughout the process of interpretation of test data, organization of a report, and actual report writing. Many of these points have been raised elsewhere (Aronow, Reznikoff, & Moreland, 1994; Tallent, 1993; Teglasi, 1992). Addressing the following issues of organization, validity, and communication satisfactorily will likely increase the usefulness of the report and render it easier to digest by the reader.

Organization

Take the time to organize the material for the report before writing it. A detailed outline is a tremendous asset in that it helps the writer to see relationships among the different domains of the subject's functioning. Contradictions in the data may emerge, and can be reconciled at this point. "Explanatory hypotheses" should be formulated based on the interpretive analyses. These explain the reasons for the subject's feelings, relationships, and conflicts, and foster understanding of the presenting problems (Teglasi, 1992). One should try to clarify the findings and create an integrated, complete picture of the individual subject. A string of statements that are not related to each other should be avoided. While organizing the report, the writer decides which interpretations to include and exclude; evaluates how much emphasis to place on them, based on their relative importance; and synthesizes the findings into a coherent summary of the person tested.

Maximizing Validity

There are several aspects of report writing that influence the validity of the end product. It is important to remember to integrate findings with the subject's history, background information, and life events. The test report should not appear to have been written in a vacuum, but rather in the context of an individual's life. Consider alternative explanations for the subject's responses and behavior. Including the subject's perspective helps increase understanding of the individual (Teglasi, 1992). Remember to include the subject's areas of strength, not only pathology.

A difficult aspect of report writing that pertains to the validity of the report is the confidence with which interpretive statements, diagnostic impressions, and recommendations are made. Language chosen should appropriately reflect the level of certainty of the examiner in making statements about the subject. For example, the writer should choose carefully among phrases such as, "it may be that," "it appears that," "evidence suggests that," "it is quite certain that," or "there is strong indication that." The choice should be based on the availability of supporting data, principally test material, but other information as well. Overinterpretation of data and unwarranted authoritative statements reflect irresponsible use of the test materials and the examiner's role. It can be appropriate to offer speculations, but they should always be labeled as such.

Caution should also be taken not to err on the opposite extreme, expressing too little confidence in one's findings. Writers who hedge too much undermine their own work by making it appear that the report is purely speculative and basically of no use at all. Evaluating one's own level of certainty when presenting interpretations and opinions is one of the most difficult aspects of report writing for the novice, and even for the more experienced psychologist. Feedback from supervisors should be helpful in striking an appropriate balance between over- and underconfidence.

Optimize Communication

A psychological test report that is logically presented and easily read and understood, will obviously have the greatest impact. One of the issues affecting the readability of the report is whether to, and, if so, how to include raw data and technical terms. The following guidelines will help the report flow with minimal interruption. It is recommended that the individual tested should always be the major focus with raw data from the test material, such as quotes and examples, primarily used to support interpretations and hypotheses. This material should not be the central topic of discussion. If tests were formally scored, scores can be reported in a separate section, either before the interpretation of the results, or in an appendix. Technical terms should usually be avoided.

The writer should keep in mind the setting in which the report is written and the audience for whom the report is written. Are the potential readers familiar with psychological assessment instruments and psychological terms? Will the report be available only to professionals, or to the subject, or to the family of the subject? These questions will guide word choice in many instances. Specific technical data, such as scores and ratios, should only be cited when the report is written in a learning context.

Another common issue that arises in report writing has to do with the appropriate length for psychological reports. Obviously, there is no hard and fast rule regarding report length. Acceptable length commonly varies with the working culture of the setting for which the report is written. More important than length are good organization, focus, and relevance. However, complaints by readers that reports are too long clearly outnumber resentments about brevity (Tallent, 1993). Reports that are too long run the risk of not being read, only having the summary section read, or, at minimum, not being read carefully. Important findings can be diluted by being immersed in too much relatively trivial or tangential material. This risk can be reduced by carefully tailoring the report to the referral question, and only adding other findings that are particularly striking. Avoiding wordiness is advised (see Williams, 1989, for excellent instruction in clear, concise writing).

Finally, reports should always be carefully proofread for errors in spelling, syntax, and grammar. These kinds of mistakes take away from the professionalism of the report and can make the content seem unreliable as well. One should proofread beyond using spell-check and grammar-check programs of word processing programs.

Computer-Generated Reports

It is becoming more common to use computers to automate various aspects of psychological assessment. While computers initially were used for the more straightforward tasks of administration and scoring, they later began to be used for the more clinical tasks of interpretation and report writing. The first computerized interpretation of tests began at the Mayo Clinic, for the MMPI (Rome, Mataya, Pearson, Swenson, & Brannick, 1965). A computerized interpretation system for a projective test, the Rorschach, was developed by Piotrowski (1964). Exner (1974) also developed a computerized interpretation system for the Rorschach based on his Comprehensive System.

The present chapter would be remiss if it did not briefly address computer-generated psychological reports, although, at this time, we are unaware of any programs that interpret the TAT or write reports including TAT material. Current standards state that final responsibility for the quality and validity of the reports lies with practitioners who use such reports (American Psychological Association, 1966); therefore, it is important for testers and consumers of psychological assessment services to be aware of the popular controversies in this area. Issues that commonly arise in consideration of computer-generated reports include whether computers "dehumanize" the assessment process, ethical implications, qualifications for use of these reports, and the validity of the reports (see Fowler, 1985, for a discussion of each of these issues).

Most computer-generated reports are either: (a) descriptions of obtained scores, (b) modeled after the judgmental process of expert test interpreters, or (c) based on statistical prediction (Butcher, Keller, & Bacon, 1985). The descriptive reports are basically summaries that do not stray far from the test data. They save time for the examiner while minimizing a more subjective interpretative process; however, their simplicity may not be sufficient for answering more complex referral questions. Computer reports that attempt to mimic high-quality interpretations of skilled clinicians can be potentially very useful; however, this assumes that the methods can be adequately translated into a computer program (Hofer & Green, 1985). It is important to know which type of interpretation—clinical or actuarial—is used when selecting a computerized system of report writing.

While the advantages of computer-generated reports are noteworthy (efficiency, potential for high quality, avoidance of individual biases of examiner), there are disadvantages of which users of these programs should be aware. Delegating administration to a computer deprives the examiner of important observations of the subject's behavior that can provide information regarding his or her relatedness, attention, motivation, and self-statements. Attention should be paid to the differences caused by various modes of test administration, such as anxiety in subjects not familiar with computers (Hofer & Green, 1985).

There are dangers of computer-generated reports that stem from the relative ease of availability of the programs. While they should not be used by unqualified persons, there is no clear policy defining minimum qualifications. It has been purported that the reports should only be used by those who would be otherwise qualified to interpret test data—so that he or she can critically evaluate the appropriateness of the reports for the individual client—taking into consideration norms, background information, and new research (Hofer & Green, 1985).

Several considerations are relevant to choosing to use a computer-assisted testing system. The user should consider the credentials of the system's author, the population on which the system was developed, and scholarly reviews of the system, and then should conduct brief trials using the system on subjects well known to the user (Moreland, 1992). Moreland cautions that computer-assisted test interpretations are not good at predicting rare events, and are not adept at interpreting unusual clinical profiles. Clinicians using these programs should also be critical of interpretations based on scores that are near cutoff scores. In general, we advocate the view that computer-generated test interpretations may be an efficient testing tool in the hands of a skilled clinician, if used carefully and critically. However, validity studies are sorely lacking at this point.

9

CHAPTER

Sample Protocols

☐ Protocol # 1

The first subject is a 15-year-old white male (Bill J.) who was referred for psychological testing in connection with decisions that needed to be made about his diagnosis and medication. He had been in psychotherapy off and on for many years, being treated for depression. Recently there had been some acting out of anger in a violent way in his family and also with friends. His school grades had also deteriorated in the past year. His present therapist suspected a possible underlying psychotic disorder in addition to depression, which was the precipitating factor for the present testing. The patient was administered the TAT as part of a full battery of tests, including the Rorschach Technique, the Figure Drawing Test, and others.

Card 1

The kid looks like his violin broke, and he's sad over it—he's torturing himself by looking at the violin. I guess he dropped it, and he's mad at himself. He's looking at it so that he can punish himself, torture himself for dropping it. (How does it work out?) He's not going to get a new violin.

He's afraid that he'll drop it again. He had a great talent, but now he'll never play it again.

Summary: A very talented boy drops his violin, wants to torture himself for this, and never plays again.

Card 2

This looks like a young woman and her mother. It looks like the mother is getting in the way of the young woman. The young woman doesn't want the mother to get into her life anymore. There's a servant in the background. The mother thinks that the girl and him will fall in love. The mother doesn't want it to happen. The young girl hates the mother, but she doesn't want to show it. She's going somewhere with her books. She's going off to do her own thing, not what the mother told her to do. The mother knows what she is doing, she enjoys making her daughter mad. She's sitting back and smiling. (How does it work out?) They'll always hate each other. When she moves out, she'll never like her mother or see much of her mother.

Summary: A mother enjoys blocking her daughter's aspiration, the daughter moves out, and they always hate each other.

Card 3BM

This looks like a woman crying on her bed. It looks like the woman is married to a guy who is abusing her. She can't divorce him and she doesn't know what to do. She's afraid she'll be with him the rest of her life, which she probably will.

Summary: A crying woman married to an abusive man is afraid to leave him.

Card 6BM

This guy looks like he's angered—he knows that he did something wrong to his mother—he's depressed that he did it and sorry but he doesn't want to say anything. The woman never saw her son act this way—it's a surprise to her. He feels bad but he won't apologize. He doesn't want to give in. He won't apologize to his mom but she knows that he's apologetic at the moment.

Summary: A man did something wrong to his mother but doesn't want to apologize.

Card 7BM

These two guys are scum—they're involved in some illegal act. They're just whispering something, to do something—"We'll do something illegal, and get a lot of money." The guy at the bottom doesn't want to do it, he looks rebellious but he knows that they'll kill him if he doesn't. The old guy looks like he's been doing it all his life. He knows the younger guy will get in trouble, but he doesn't care.

Summary: Two criminals are planning a crime, and the older one doesn't care if the younger one gets in trouble.

Card 13B

This kid lives in a poor home—the family doesn't want him in the house. He wants to go some place where he can think things over. When he gets money, his parents take it away from him. He'll be rich and famous as an adult and they'll want help and he won't help them. He has friends so that's how he gets by this period of his life.

Summary: Parents don't want to help a poor child and when he becomes successful he doesn't help them.

Card 13MF

This guy looks like he just killed his wife—no, he walked into the room and saw his wife dead. He's about to call the police. His life will be messed up from then on because of this tragic thing that happened to him. (How does it work out?) He'll be depressed for the rest of his life—he'll live like a hermit.

Summary: A man finds his wife dead and never recovers from it.

Card16

There are two young kids arguing, it looks like they're about to get into a huge fight. The kids will beat the crap out of each other. Probably one will die, and his family will get revenge and kill the other one and then everything will be even.

Summary: Two children fight and one dies, then the family gets revenge.

Interpretation

In this patient's TAT stories, certain themes repeat themselves. The stories depict situations of failure (notably card 1); conflict with almost everyone, but particularly with authority figures; and a depressive, pessimistic, hopeless outlook regarding the future.

At one point anger is seen as directed inward (card 1) and at another point the patient is able to change a story in which the male protagonist is violent to a story in which he is not (13MF). In one card, some tenderness toward the mother figure is expressed (card 6BM). Remarks on card 1 ("torturing himself") suggest a directing of anger inward. Lack of confidence in the self is also pronounced (card 1). The very strong and somewhat perseverative view of others as highly negative toward him suggests that projection is being used. A general view of the parents as malevolent is apparent (cards 2, 13B). Peers are seen in more positive terms (card 13B).

It should be noted that in other tests (notably the Rorschach) administered to this patient extensive use of projection is seen as well as generally poor ego-functioning consistent with psychosis. The general diagnostic impression is one of Schizophrenia, Paranoid Type.

☐ Protocol # 2[1]

The following test record was obtained from a 76-year-old woman who volunteered as a test subject, thus giving us a test record of a senior to evaluate. She expressed appreciation for the company of the examiner. It was necessary on several occasions to remind her of the basic questions to be considered in constructing a story and reassure her that there were no correct answers. She appeared to have some minor difficulty with visual activity that may have influenced the detail of her responses.

---

[1] Many thanks are expressed to Lisa Tischler, M.A., of Fordham University for providing protocol # 2.

Card 1

I don't know what this object is. He's concentrating on this object. He seems to be concentrating very hard on it, maybe figuring out what it is. He has free time on his hands. He's just sitting amusing himself. He's absorbed with it. He may see something that I don't see. He's relaxed, he's thinking. He may figure out what it is, but I don't know what it is. But he looks like he's looking at something he understands. If he's bright he'll figure it out.

(Additional reading of directions at this point.)

Summary: Someone is looking at something, patiently trying to figure it out.

Card 2

This takes place on a farm. Farmer with a horse, seeding the ground. This must be the young daughter with school books. His wife is watching him. Horse to help with seeding. She may be going to school because she has books. Not 12 or 13, 19 or upper teens. The more mature woman could be mom relaxing up against a tree. Field looks like a hard days work, it looks well done. He did the field and accomplished what he set out to do in making the ground fully plowed.

Summary: A farm scene with a family going about their business.

Card 3BM

Looks like a very depressed female. She may be mental, or just depressed. She doesn't look sick, she looks like she's hurting. Whether she'll get help, and someone will make her feel good—I don't know. She's resting with her head on the bench and she looks unhappy. Maybe she had a hard day, she doesn't look sick or abused. Maybe abused, but she doesn't show her face so I don't know what led up to it. I hope something good happens to her. If I could see her face, I may know, and read into her. I don't know the outcome.

Summary: A depressed female is hurting and looking unhappy.

Card 3GF

The male or female looks very unhappy. Something awful must have happened to her. She's weeping and stooped over. Not abused, just an unhappy individual. Maybe she had an argument but she's not beaten. Whether going back into the house to smooth over what happened. . . . Decided she's going back in. Don't know if going in or out. Goes in and smoothes it over. They make up and have a good evening.

Summary: An unhappy woman is weeping then goes back in and makes up.

Card 4

These two are a male and a female in an argument. He's angry at her and she's trying to pacify him. He won't give an inch. She may wind up winning him over because she's looking at him endearingly. She wants harmony in the relationship and is sorry about what happened. She will try harder to win him back. I think she'll get him back. He isn't that angry, and she's looking at him endearingly. She'll get him back.

Summary: A man and woman have an argument and she wins him over with endearing looks.

Card 6BM

This looks like it could be mom and son in some deep conversation. Both look very unhappy though he's looking out the window. He's unhappy, his eyes are downcast. They could be discussing lifestyles. Maybe she doesn't like his friends, or his job, or his wife. Anything. He looks unhappy. We hope that they will work it out, but he's very unhappy right now. He'll make up with his mom and it will be love and bliss again.

Summary: A mother doesn't like her son's lifestyle, but they make up.

Card 7BM

Two men, don't represent anything. Not dad and son, maybe employee and employer—very absorbed and discussing something of great importance. Very serious. Will win the case. Could be attorneys.

Summary: Two men discuss something important.

Card 8BM

This looks like war. Gun here and surgeon and operation, and assistant, and this dressed fellow. So maybe it's not a war scene. Operation on someone. There's a gun in the picture. This is maybe a bullet wound. They are working earnestly. The gentleman on the table is half covered, and the guy is with a knife cutting into him, but the gentleman here is misleading. If the guy here wasn't here, it would be a war scene. You see the gun here. I don't know, the patient will live.

   Summary: Someone is being operated on, and survives.

Card 13MF

He's got clothes on, so it's not a sexual thing. She's half dressed in bed. Maybe he abused her, he's holding his eyes. Don't know if he will change his mind, be a nice guy and make love to her. He looks sorry. He's covering his eyes and face. So he could have abused her, or hurt her. No indications of what he will do. Maybe she's a prostitute. He seems ashamed. He looks like he's going to leave.

   Summary: A man hurts a woman and is ashamed and sorry.

Interpretation

The general impression is one of emotional functioning that is within the normal range. This client does approach environmental situations with caution and uncertainty, feeling that she must expend considerable effort and concentration on interpreting them objectively and correctly (card 1). She characteristically appears to search for inconsistencies and illogicalities in her perceptions to be confident that she has judged social interactions accurately (cards 8BM, 13MF). She strongly identifies with the role of an effective peacemaker in her dealings with males, whom she experiences as typically stubborn; at times, irrationally angry; and as having rather conflicted abusive proclivities (cards 3BM, 3GF, 13MF).

   As reflected in the client's tendency to assign happy endings to many of her stories, denial and avoidance are central defenses in dealing with her occasionally overwhelming dysphoric emotions (card 3BM). She feels that seeking help for her negative feelings might be appropriate and that "someone might make her feel good."

   Her conception of the family is a basically traditional one (card 2). Mother-child contacts are seen as sometimes friction laden, resulting from a critical maternal view of an offspring's lifestyle. In her view, however, such disagreements can be successfully resolved with a resultant positive relationship (card 6BM).

At the present time, this client feels rather uncertain in dealing with environmental demands. She typically endeavors to counter negative emotions by denying and distancing herself from them. Her longtime self-image is that of an effective conciliator, particularly in her interactions with angry, potentially abusive males. Her description of the figure in card 1 as having "free time on his hands" is likely a self-projection.

☐ Protocol # 3

Following is a TEMAS protocol of a 5-year-old Hispanic (Puerto Rican) male who had been brought to a mental health clinic by his mother with complaints of aggressiveness and hyperactivity. He is the youngest of three children, having moved to the mainland with his family when he was 3. He lives with his parents and his siblings. The mother states that he has aggressive outbursts and injures himself by scratching his face and arms; he is also described as initiating physical fights with his 8-year-old sister during which he pulls her hair.

The client is in kindergarten and appears to have a speech difficulty since he is unable to express himself fluently even in Spanish. The Spanish-speaking examiner had difficulty understanding what he was saying at times; at those times, the client reacted with impatience and annoyance. The administration was in Spanish.

Card 10B

(Boy with money and a piggy bank, imagining a bicycle in a shop window and buying ice cream).

The boy found the animal (pig, which in the card is a piggy bank). He wants to sell it. He feels sad because he found the animal. Here he is buying an ice cream with the money. He likes ice cream. Look, here he is looking at a bicycle and he is sad because he wants to buy it, but he can't. That's it!

Summary: A boy finds an animal, wants to buy things, and is sad when he can't.

Card 11

(A woman with grocery bags is being helped by a boy and a girl. Another woman is protecting herself from children stealing her groceries).

The kids stole something. Here's a cane. These other ones did the same thing—look. They want to go into the house (both groups of children), but the ladies don't want to go in because they already were there. They already went in to steal (the ladies). Look—they took milk. I don't know how they are feeling. I don't know what is going to happen to them.

Summary: People are stealing things (chaotic story).

Card 17B

(A boy who is studying dreams about getting an "A" from the teacher, or getting an "F").

He is looking at a book (speaking about the boy sitting at a desk) and he is also looking here (pointing to the boy who had an F on the paper). He is very sad because of the man. This one here (the boy who had an A on the paper) is also sad. I don't know why. The boy is sad because he has a lot of homework. I have a lot of homework in school. That's it.

Summary: A boy is sad (chaotic story).

Card 19B

(A boy in a window pictures himself being saved by a fireman and by Superman).

The kid is sad because this one is flying and he can't. Look at the fireman. He is going up the ladder to help him down because of the fire. He is going to get burned. Look at the fire. I don't know how it happened.

Summary: A boy is sad because he can't fly, while a fireman is trying to help him.

Card 20

(A kid in bed dreams of a scene with a river, a horse, and a castle).

I don't want to do anymore! The kid took off his clothes. The horse is jumping and wants to go up to the house. The boy is thinking about the horse because he wants to ride it. I don't know what he is feeling. This is his horse and he wants to ride it. Look at the mountains.

Summary: A boy takes off his clothes and he wants to ride his horse.

Card 21

(A child dreams of two monsters—one eating something, the other threatening).

He (the child) is scared because the monster is bad. This one is eating but is also bad. Look, this one is throwing fire. The monster is bad. He wants to throw fire to him (pointing to the boy in the bed) because he is a bad monster. The boy is dreaming and he is going to get food from this one (pointing to the dragon who is eating). The boy is scared of the monsters. I don't know what else.

Summary: A boy is afraid of a monster throwing fire and wants food from another monster.

Interpretation

The dominant impression of this young boy's stories is of the children in them who are consistently sad, helpless, or who behave aggressively. In fact, in cards 10B, 17B, and 19B the actual feeling of "sadness" is one of the first things mentioned in the story. On card 17B, the child is sad regardless of his facial expression. An underlying depression is suggested.

The theme of aggression is also prominent in this client's stories. The aggression may be expressed by the story's main character (card 11) or may be inflicted on the main character (card 21). This is likely related to the home environment. In this connection, it should be noted that both monsters are described as "bad" on card 21, intent on hurting the child. Impulsivity and impatience are also suggested by the child's highly verbal expression of not wanting to continue.

☐ Protocol # 4

The following is not a complete TAT test protocol, but only the response to card 14 by a female college student who was also a talented writer and who, tragically, committed suicide subsequent to the test administration.

Card 14

Now I am free. The darkness of my room has liberated me to the darkness outside, a bright black indeed in comparison with the shadow that clouds the objects I live amongst daily. This time of night is what I walk through the motions of school for, each long morning and afternoon. Now that the dormitory has ceased its racket of shouting, toothbrushing, and algebra, and the teachers relaxed their roles as caretakers, I can leave the institutional walls and halls for the regions beyond that never dreamt of either structure. Only the windows I love in this maze of a building, for letting me out to the structureless sky. And yet I feel it is not quite structureless, I feel shapes, configurations, forms without description, existing and moving in modes wholly incomprehensible to the earth-seeing mind. Then that earth dims out, its patterns reduced to the irrelevant, its noise barely felt. All importance and all actual existence is here, in watching and speculating wordlessly on the depths above, in waiting for and almost working for a further window, through which to see with a totally new concept of perception the actuality that now mists beyond my comprehension. I work for it, I struggle to find the new paths to send my mind down, but they remain strange to me. Perhaps all this effort is useless here, perhaps my human existence precludes true knowledge of what I cannot grasp yet. Surely if it were possible, someone in all the reels of time played out would have found it and left some word. But what I've read of those who claim to have achieved union with the infinite or other mystical experience of that nature means nothing to what I see—almost see—feel dimly out beyond. The only beyond that living men know nothing of, that no tales return from and no book describes, that is not bound by instinctive rationality and needs for preservation, is death. That may be the transition, where human habits that here block my sight may be cast off with human individuality and separateness, and actual communion of all occur. If not, well, I won't *know*, as I now know what's for supper and feel glad or disappointed, for that mental faculty too will be gone. All gone, leaving—perhaps—just the core, the essence of existence and reality. It's a good enough gamble. And this window is high enough.

REFERENCES

Aaron, N. S. (1967). Some personality differences between asthmatics, allergic, and normal children. *Journal of Clinical Psychology, 23*, 336–340.

American Psychiatric Association. (1994). *Diagnostic and statistical manual of mental disorders* (4th ed.). Washington, DC: Author.

American Psychological Association. (1966). Interim standards for automated test scoring and interpretation practices. *American Psychologist, 22*, 1141.

American Psychological Association. (1992). Ethical principles for psychologists and code of conduct. *American Psychologist, 47*, 1597–1611.

Anderson, J. W. (1999). Henry A. Murray and the creation of the Thematic Apperception Test. In L. Geiser & M. I. Stein (Eds.), *Evocative images* (pp. 23–38). Washington, DC: American Psychological Association.

Andor, L. E. (1983). *Psychological and sociological studies of the Black people of Africa, south of the Sahara 1960–1975—An annotated select bibliography*. Johannesburg, South Africa: National Institute for Personnel Research.

Appelbaum, S. A. (1990). The relationship between assessment and psychotherapy. *Journal of Personality Assessment, 54*, 791–801.

Araoz, D. L. (1972). The Thematic Apperception Test in marital therapy. *Journal of Contemporary Psychotherapy, 5*, 41–48.

Aronow, E., & Reznikoff, M. (1971). Application of projective tests to psychotherapy: A case study. *Journal of Personality Assessment, 35*, 379–393.

Aronow, E., Reznikoff, M., & Moreland, K. (1994). *The Rorschach technique*. Needham Heights, MA: Allyn & Bacon.

Atkinson, J. W., & Feather, N. T. (Eds.). (1966). *A theory of achievement motivation*. New York: Wiley.

Bailey, B. E., & Green, J. (1977). Black thematic apperception test stimulus material. *Journal of Personality Assessment, 41*, 25–30.

Baty, M. A. & Dreger, R. M. (1975). A comparison of three methods to record TAT protocols. *Journal of Clinical Psychology, 31*, 348.

Bellak, L., & Abrams, D. M. (1997). *The TAT, CAT, and SAT in clinical use* (6th ed.). Boston: Allyn & Bacon.

Bellak L., Abrams, D. M., & Ackermann-Engel, R. (1992*). Handbook of intensive brief and emergency psychotherapy*. Larchmont, NY: C.P.S.

Bellak, L., & Bellak, S. S. (1948). *The CAT*. Larchmont, NY: C.P.S.

Bellak, L., & Bellak, S. S. (1965). *The CAT-H: A human modification*. Larchmont, NY: C.P.S.

Bellak, L., & Bellak, S. S. (1973). *The SAT*. Larchmont, NY: C.P.S.

Bellak, L., & Hurvich, M. (1966). A human modification of the Children's Apperception Test. *Journal of Projective Techniques, 30*, 228–242.

Berends, A., Westen, D., Leigh, J., & Silbert, D. (1990). Assessing affect-tone of relationship paradigms from TAT and interview data. *Psychological Assessment, 2,* 329–332.

Bernstein, E., & Perry, J. C. (1995). *A TAT analysis of object relations in Borderline, Antisocial, Schizotypal, and Bipolar II disorders.* Unpublished manuscript, Boston University.

Binet, A. & Henri, V. (1896). La psychologie individuelle. *Annee Psychologique, 2,* 411–465.

Birney, R. C., (1968). Research on the achievement motive. In E. F. Borgatta & W. W. Lambert (Eds.), *Handbook of personality theory and research.* Chicago: Rand McNally.

Blum, G. S. (1950). *The Blacky pictures: Manual of instructions.* New York: Psychological Corporation.

Butcher, J. N. (1990). *MMPI–2 in psychological treatment.* New York: Oxford University Press.

Butcher, J. N., Keller, L. S., & Bacon, S. F. (1985). Current developments and future directions in computerized personality assessment. *Journal of Consulting and Clinical Psychology, 53,* 803–815.

Butcher, J. N., & Pancheri, P. (1976). *A handbook of cross-national MMPI research.* Minneapolis, MN: University of Minnesota Press.

Canter, M. B., Bennett, B. E., Jones, S. E., & Nagy, T. F. (1994). *Ethics for psychologists: A commentary on the APA ethics code.* Washington, DC: American Psychological Association.

Chowdhury, U. (1960a). *An Indian adaptation of the Children's Apperception Test.* Delhi, India: Manasayan.

Chowdhury, U. (1960b). An Indian modification of the Thematic Apperception Test. *The Journal of Social Psychology, 51,* 245–263.

Coche, E., & Sillitti, J. A. (1983). The Thematic Apperception Test in an outcome measure in psychotherapy research. *Psychotherapy, Theory, Research and Practice, 20,* 41–46.

Combs, A. (1946). The use of personal experience in Thematic Apperception Test story plots. *Journal of Clinical Psychology, 2,* 357–363.

Costantino, G., Malgady, R. G., Casullo, M. M., & Castillo, A. (1991). Cross-cultural standardization of TEMAS in three Hispanic subcultures. *Hispanic Journal of Behavioral Sciences, 13,* 48–62.

Costantino, G., Malgady, R. G., Rogler, L. H., & Tsui, E. C. (1988). Discriminant analysis of clinical outpatients and public school children by TEMAS: A Thematic Apperception Test for Hispanics and Blacks. *Journal of Personality Assessment, 52,* 670–678.

Costantino, G., Malgady, R. G., & Vazquez, C. (1981). A comparison of the Murray-TAT and a new Thematic Apperception Test for urban Hispanic children. *Hispanic Journal of Behavioral Sciences, 3,* 291–300.

Cowan, G., & Goldberg, F. J. (1967). Need achievement as a function of the race and sex of figures of selected TAT cards. *Journal of Personality and Social Psychology, 5,* 245–249.

Craddick, R. A. (1972). Humanistic assessment: A reply to Brown. *Psychotherapy: Theory, Research and Practice, 9,* 107–110.

Craddick, R. A. (1975). Sharing oneself in the assessment procedure. *Professional Psychology, 6,* 279–282.

Cramer, P. (1987). The development of defense mechanisms. *Journal of Personality, 55,* 597–614.

Cramer, P. (1990). *The development of defense mechanisms: Theory, research, and assessment.* New York: Springer-Verlag.

Cramer, P., Blatt, S. J., & Ford, R. Q. (1988). Defense mechanisms in the anaclitic and introjective personality configuration. *Journal of Consulting and Clinical Psychology, 56,* 610–616.

Cramer, P., & Block, J. (1998). Preschool antecedents of defense mechanism use in young adults: A longitudinal study. *Journal of Personality and Social Psychology, 74,* 159–169.

Dana, R. H. (1985). Thematic Apperception Test. In C. S. Newmark (Ed.), *Major psychological assessment instruments* (pp. 89–134). Newton, MA: Allyn & Bacon.

Dana, R. H. (1996). The Thematic Apperception Test (TAT). In C. S. Newmark (Ed.), *Major psychological assessment instruments* (2nd ed., pp. 166–205). Needham Heights, MA: Allyn & Bacon.

Dana, R. H. (1999). Cross-cultural/multicultural use of the Thematic Apperception Test. In M. Geiser & M. Stein (Eds.), *Evocative images.* Washington, DC: American Psychological Association.

Davids, A., & Rosenblatt, D. (1958). Use of the TAT in assessment of alienation. *Journal of Projective Techniques, 22,* 145–152.

Deplu, O., & Kimbrough, C. (1982). Feeling-tone and card preferences of Black elementary children for the TCB and TAT. *Journal of Non-White Concerns, 10,* 50–56.

Douglas, C. (1993). *Translate the darkness: The life of Christiana Morgan.* New York: Simon & Schuster.

Dymond, R. F. (1954). Adjustment changes over therapy from Thematic Apperception Test ratings. In C. R. Rogers & R. F. Dymond (Eds.), *Psychotherapy and personality change* (pp. 76–84). Chicago: University of Chicago Press.

Erasmus, P. F. (1975). *TAT-Z catalogue no. 1676.* Pretoria, Human Sciences Research Council.

Eron, L. D. (1950). A normative study of the Thematic Apperception Test. *Psychological Monographs, 64*(9, Whole No. 315).

Eron, L. D. (1953). Responses of women to the Thematic Apperception Test. *Journal of Consulting Psychology, 17,* 269–282.

Exner, J. E., Jr. (1974). *The Rorschach: A comprehensive system* (Vol. 1). New York: Wiley.

Fairweather, G., Simon, R., Gebhard, M., Weingarten, E., Holland, J., Sanders, R., Stone, G., & Reahl, J. (1960). Relative effectiveness of psychotherapeutic programs: A multicriteria comparison of four programs for three different patient groups. *Psychology Monographs, 74*(5).

Finn, S. E., & Tonsager, M. E. (1992). Therapeutic effects of providing MMPI-2 test feedback to college students awaiting therapy. *Psychological Assessment, 4,* 278–287.

Fischer, C. T. (1970). The testee as co-evaluator. *Journal of Counseling Psychology, 17,* 70–76.

Fischer, C. T. (1972). Paradigm changes which allow sharing of results. *Professional Psychology, 3,* 365–369.

Fisher, S. & Hinds, E. (1951). The organization of hostility controls in various personality structures. *Genetic Psychological Monographs, 44,* 3–68.

Fowler, R. D. (1985). Landmarks in computer-assisted psychological assessment. *Journal of Consulting and Clinical Psychology, 53,* 748–759.

Frank, A. F., & Gunderson, J. G. (1990). The role of the therapeutic alliance in the treatment of schizophrenia: Relationship to course and outcome. *Archives of General Psychiatry, 47,* 228–236.

French, L. A. (1993). Adapting projective tests for minority children. *Psychological Reports, 72,* 15–18.

Gass, C. S., & Brown, M. C. (1992). Neuropsychological test feedback to patients with brain dysfunction. *Psychological Assessment, 4,* 272–277.

Goldfried, M., & Zax, M. (1965). The stimulus value of the TAT. *Journal of Projective Techniques, 29,* 46–57.

Goldman, R., & Greenblatt, M. (1955). Changes in Thematic Apperception Test stories paralleling changes in clinical status of schizophrenic patients. *Journal of Nervous and Mental Diseases, 121,* 243–249.

Hafner, A. J., & Kaplan, A. M. (1960). Hostility content analysis of the Rorschach and TAT. *Journal of Projective Techniques, 24,* 137–143.

Harrison, R. (1965). Thematic apperceptive methods. In B. Wolman (Ed.), *Handbook of clinical psychology* (pp. 562–620). New York: McGraw Hill.

Harrower, M. (1960). Projective counseling—A psychotherapeutic technique. In M. Harrower (Ed.), *Creative variations in the projective techniques.* Springfield, IL: Thomas.

Hartman, A. H. (1970). A basic TAT set. *Journal of Personality Assessment, 34*, 391–396.

Haskell, R. J., Jr. (1961). Relationship between aggressive behavior and psychological tests. *Journal of Projective Techniques, 25*, 431–440.

Haskin, P. R. (1958). *A study of the relationship between realistic and unrealistic aggression, reliance on categorical attitudes, and constructiveness of adjustment.* Unpublished doctoral dissertation, Western Reserve University.

Hibbard, S., Farmer, L., Wells, C., DiFillipo, E., Barry, W., Korman, R., & Sloan, P. (1994). Validation of Cramer's defense mechanism manual for the TAT. *Journal of Personality Assessment, 63*, 197–210.

Hibbard, S., Hilsenroth, M. J., Hibbard, J. K., & Nash, M. R. (1995). A validity study of two projective object representations measures. *Psychological Assessment, 7*, 432–439.

Hofer, P. J., & Green, B. F. (1985). The challenge of competence and creativity in computerized psychological testing. *Journal of Consulting and Clinical Psychology, 53*, 826–838.

Hoffman, S., & Kuperman, N. (1990). Indirect treatment of traumatic psychological experiences: The use of TAT cards. *American Journal of Psychotherapy, 44*, 107–115.

Holmstrom, R. W., Silber, D. E., & Karp, S. A. (1990). Development of the Apperceptive Personality Test. *Journal of Personality Assessment, 54*, 252–264.

Holzberg, J. (1963). Projective techniques and resistance to change in psychotherapy as viewed through a communications model. *Journal of Projective Techniques, 27*, 430–435.

Hutt, M. L. (1980). *The Michigan Picture Test-Revised: Manual.* New York: Grune & Stratton.

James, P. B., & Mosher, D. L. (1967). Thematic aggression, hostility-guilt, and aggressive behavior. *Journal of Projective Techniques and Personality Assessment, 31*(1), 61–67.

Jung, C. G. (1961). *Memories, dreams, and reflections* (A. Jaffe, Ed.). New York: Pantheon.

Kahn, M. (1984). The usefulness of the TAT blank card in clinical practice. *Psychotherapy in Private Practice, 2*, 43–50.

Karon, B. P. (1981). The Thematic Apperception Test. In A. I. Rabin (Ed.), *Assessment with projective techniques* (pp. 85–120). New York: Springer.

Katz, H. E., Russ, S. W., & Overholser, J. C. (1993). Sex differences, sex roles, and projection on the TAT: Matching stimulus to examinee gender. *Journal of Personality Assessment, 60*, 186–191.

Klopfer, B., & Kelley, D. M. (1946). *The Rorschach technique.* Yonkers, NY: World Book Company.

Korchin, S. J., Mitchell, H. E., & Meltzoff, J. (1950). A critical evaluation of the Thompson Thematic Apperception Test. *Journal of Projective Techniques, 14*, 445–451.

Lefkowitz, J. & Fraser, A. W. (1980). Assessment of achievement and power motivation of Blacks and Whites, using a Black and White TAT, with Black and White administrators. *Journal of Applied Psychology, 65*, 685–696.

Lubin, B., Larsen, R. M., & Matarazzo, J. D. (1984). Patterns of psychological test usage in the United States: 1935–1982. *American Psychologist, 39*, 451–454.

Malgady, R. G., Costantino, G., & Rogler, L. H. (1984). Development of a Thematic Apperception Test (TEMAS) for urban Hispanic children. *Journal of Consulting and Clinical Psychology, 52*, 986–996.

McArthur, D. S., & Roberts, G. E. (1982). *Roberts Apperception Test for Children: A manual.* Los Angeles: Western Psychological Services.

McClelland, D. C. (1958). Risk taking in children with high and low need for achievement. In J. W. Atkinson (Ed.), *Motives in fantasy, action, and society.* Princeton, NJ: Van Nostrand.

McClelland, D. C. (1961a). *The achieving society.* New York: Van Nostrand.

McClelland, D. C. (1961b). Encouraging excellence. *Daedalus, 90*, 711–724.

McClelland, D. C. (1965). Achievement and entrepreneurship: A longitudinal study. *Journal of Personality and Social Psychology, 1*, 389–391.

McClelland, D. C. (1995). Achievement motivation in relation to achievement-related recall, performance and urine flow, a marker associated with release of vasopressin.

Motivation and Emotion, 19, 59–76.

McClelland, D. C., Atkinson, J. W., Clark, R. A., & Lowell, E. L. (1953). *The achievement motive.* New York: Appleton-Century-Crofts.

McClelland, D. C., Koestner, R., & Weinberger, J. (1989). How do self-attributed and implicit motives differ? *Psychological Review, 96,* 690–702.

McClelland, D. C., & Pilon, D. A. (1983). Sources of adult motives in patterns of parent behavior in early childhood. *Journal of Personality and Social Psychology, 44,* 564–574.

McGaugh, J. L. (1990). Significance and remembrance: The role of neuromodulatory systems. *Psychological Science, 1,* 15–25.

Megargee, E. I. (1967). Hostility on the TAT as a function of defensive inhibition and stimulus situation. *Journal of Projective Techniques, 31,* 73–79.

Megargee, E. I. & Cook, P. E. (1967). The relation of TAT and inkblot aggressive content scales with each other and with criteria or overt aggression in juvenile delinquents. *Journal of Projective Techniques and Personality Assessment, 31,* 48–60.

Millon, T. (1987). *Manual for the MCMI-II* (2nd ed.). Minneapolis, MN: National Computer Systems.

Moreland, K. L. (1992). Computer-assisted psychological assessment. In M. Zeidner & R. Most (Eds.), *Psychological testing: An inside view* (pp. 343–376). Palo Alto, CA: Consulting Psychologists Press.

Morgan, C. D., & Murray, H. A. (1935). A method for investigating fantasies: The Thematic Apperception Test. *Archives of Neurological Psychiatry, 34,* 289–306.

Morgan, W. G. (1995). Origin and history of the Thematic Apperception Test images. *Journal of Personality Assessment, 65,* 237–254.

Murray, H. A. (1943). *The Thematic Apperception Test: Plates and manual.* Cambridge, MA: Harvard University Press.

Murstein, B. I. (1959). A conceptual model of projective techniques applied to stimulus variations with thematic techniques. *Journal of Consulting Psychology, 23,* 3–14.

Murstein, B. I. (1963). *Theory and research in projective techniques.* New York: Wiley.

Murstein, B. I. (1972). Normative written TAT responses for a college sample. *Journal of Personality Assessment, 36,* 109–147.

Mussen, P., & Naylor, H. (1954). The relationships between overt and fantasy aggression. *Journal of Abnormal and Social Psychology, 49,* 235–240.

Nigg, J., Silk, K., Westen, D., Lohr, N., Gold, L., Goodrich, S., & Ogata, S. (1991). Object representations in the early memories of sexually abused borderline patients. *American Journal of Psychiatry, 148,* 864–869.

Obrzut, J. E. & Boliek, C. A. (1986). Thematic approaches to personality assessment with children and adolescents. In H. M. Knoff (Ed.), *The assessment of child and adolescent personality* (pp. 183–198). New York: Guilford.

Palomares, R. S., Crowley, S. L., Worchel, F. F., Olson, T. K., & Rae, W. A. (1991). The factor analytic structure of the Roberts Apperception Test for Children: A comparison of the standardization sample with a sample of chronically ill children. *Journal of Personality Assessment, 56,* 414–425.

Piotrowski, C. (1950). A new evaluation of the Thematic Apperception Test. *Psychoanalytic Review, 37,* 101–127.

Piotrowski, C., & Keller, J. W. (1984). Psychodiagnostic testing in APA-approved clinical psychology programs. *Professional Psychology: Research and Practice, 3,* 450–456.

Piotrowski, Z. A. (1964). A digital computer administration in inkblot test data. *Psychiatric Quarterly, 38,* 1–26.

Porcerelli, J. H., Cogan, R. & Hibbard, S. (1998). Cognitive and affective representations of people and MCMI–II personality psychopathology. *Journal of Personality Assessment, 70,* 535–540.

Porcerelli, J. H., Thomas, S., Hibbard, S., & Cogan, R. (1998). Defense mechanisms development in children, adolescents, and late adolescents. *Journal of Personality Assessment, 71,* 411–420.

Purcell, K. (1956). The TAT and antisocial behavior. *Journal of Consulting Psychology, 20,* 449–456.

Rapaport, D., Gill, M. M., & Schafer, R. (1968). *Diagnostic psychological testing.* New York: International Universities Press.

Retief, A. I. (1987). Thematic apperception testing across cultures: Tests of selection versus tests of inclusion. *South African Journal of Psychology, 17,* 47–55.

Reznikoff, M., & Dollin, A. (1961). Social desirability and the type of hostility expressed on the TAT. *Journal of Clinical Psychology, 17,* 315–317.

Ritzler, B. A., Sharkey, K. J., & Chudy, J. F. (1980). A comprehensive projective alternative to the TAT. *Journal of Personality Assessment, 44,* 358–362.

Rome, H. P., Mataya, P., Pearson, J. S., Swenson, A. Z., & Brannick, T. (1965). Automatic personality assessment. In R. W. Stacy & B. Waxman (Eds.), *Computers in biomedical research* (Vol. 1, pp. 505–524). New York: Academic Press.

Rorschach, H. (1942). *Psychodiagnostics* (5th ed., P. Lemkau & B. Kronenberg, Trans.). Berne, Switzerland: Verlag Hans Huber. (Original work published 1921).

Rosenwald, G. C. (1968). The Thematic Apperception Test. In A. I. Rabin (Ed.), *Projective techniques in personality assessment: A modern introduction* (pp. 172–221). New York: Springer.

Rosenzweig, S. H. (1948). The Thematic Apperception Test in diagnosis and therapy. *Journal of Personality, 16,* 437–444.

Rossini, E. D., & Moretti, R. J. (1997). Thematic Apperception Test (TAT) interpretation: Practice recommendations from a survey of clinical psychology doctoral programs accredited by the American Psychological Association. *Professional Psychology: Research and Practice, 28,* 393–398.

Roth, L. H., Wolford, J., & Meisel, A. (1980). Patient access to records: Tonic or toxin? *American Journal of Psychiatry, 137,* 592–596.

Sanford, R. N., et al. (1943). *Physique, personality and scholarship.* Washington, DC: Society for Research in Child Development.

Schafer, R. (1954). *Psychoanalytic interpretation in Rorschach testing.* New York: Grune & Stratton.

Scodel, A. & Lipetz, M. E. (1957). TAT hostility and psychopathology. *Journal of Projective Techniques, 21,* 161–165.

Sherwood, E. T. (1957). On the designing of TAT pictures, with special reference to a set for an African people assimilating Western culture. *The Journal of Social Psychology, 45,* 161–190.

Shneidman, E. S. (1952). *The Make-A-Picture Story Test.* New York: Psychological Corporation.

Solomon, I. L., & Starr, B. D. (1968). *School Apperception Method (SAM).* New York: Springer.

Spangler, W. D. (1992). Validity of questionnaire and TAT measures of need for achievement: Two meta-analyses. *Psychological Bulletin, 112,* 140–154.

Stein, E. J., Furedy, R. L., Simonton, M. J., & Neuffer, C. H. (1979). Patient access to medical records on a psychiatric inpatient unit. *American Journal of Psychiatry, 136,* 327–332.

Stein, M. I. (1981). *The Thematic Apperception Test* (2nd ed.). Springfield, IL: Thomas.

Stone, H., & Dellis, N. (1960). An exploratory investigation into the levels hypothesis. *Journal of Projective Techniques, 24,* 333–340.

Tallent, N. (1993). *Psychological report writing* (2nd ed.). Englewood Cliffs, NJ: Prentice-Hall.

Teglasi, H. (1992). *Clinical use of storytelling.* Boston: Allyn & Bacon.

Terry, D. (1952). The use of a rating scale of level of response in TAT stories. *Journal of Abnormal Social Psychology, 47,* 507–511.

Theiner, E. (1962). Experimental needs are expressed by projective techniques. *Journal of Projective Techniques, 26,* 354–363.

Thompson, C. E. (1949). The Thompson modification of the Thematic Apperception Test. *Journal of Projective Techniques, 17,* 469–478.

Thompson, C. E., & Bachrach, A. J. (1951). The use of color in the Thematic Apperception Test. *Journal of Projective Techniques, 15,* 173–184.

Tompkins, S. (1947). *The Thematic Apperception Test: The theory and technique of interpretation.* New York: Grune & Stratton.

Triplett, S., & Brunson, P. (1982). TCB and TAT response characteristics in Black males and females: A replication. *Journal of Non-White Concerns, 10,* 73–77.

Ullmann, L. (1957). Selection of neuropsychiatric patients for group psychotherapy. *Journal of Consulting Psychology, 21,* 277–280.

Watkins, C. E., Cambell, V. L., Nieberding, R., & Hallmark, R. (1995). Contemporary practice of psychological assessment by clinical psychologists. *Professional Psychology: Research and Practice, 26,* 54–60.

Weiner, B. (1970). New conceptions in the study of achievement motivation. In B. A. Maher (Ed.), *Progress in experimental personality research* (Vol. 5). New York: Academic Press.

Weisskopf, E. A. (1950). A transcendence index as a proposed measure in the TAT. *Journal of Psychology, 29,* 379–390.

Weisskopf-Joelson, E. A. & Foster, H. C. (1962). An experimental study of stimulus variation upon projection. *Journal of Projective Techniques, 26,* 366–370.

Weissman, S. (1964). Some indicators of acting out behavior from the Thematic Apperception Test. *Journal of Projective Techniques, 28,* 366–375.

Westen, D. (1991). Clinical assessment of object relations using the TAT. *Journal of Personality Assessment, 56,* 56–74.

Westen, D. (1995). *Revision of Social Cognition and Object Relations Scale: Q-Sort for projective stories (SCORS–Q).* Unpublished manuscript, Department of Psychiatry, Cambridge Hospital and Harvard Medical School, Cambridge, MA.

Westen, D., Klepser, J., Ruffins, S. A., Silverman, M., Lifton, N., & Boekamp, J. (1991). Object relations in childhood and adolescence: The development of working representations. *Journal of Consulting and Clinical Psychology, 59,* 400–409.

Westen, D., Lohr, N., Silk, K. R., Gold, L., & Kerber, K. (1990). Object relations and social cognition in borderlines, major depressives and normals: A Thematic Apperception Test analysis. *Psychological Assessment, 2,* 355–364.

Westen, D., Lohr, N., Silk, K., Kerber, K., & Goodrich, S. (1989). *Object relations and social cognition TAT scoring manual* (4th ed.). Unpublished manuscript, University of Michigan, Ann Arbor.

Westen, D., Ludolph, P., Block, M. J., Wixom, J., & Wiss, F. C. (1991). Developmental history and object relations in psychiatrically disturbed adolescent girls. *American Journal of Psychiatry, 148,* 1419–1420.

Williams, J. M. (1989). *Style: Ten lessons in clarity and grace* (10th ed.). Boston: Scott, Foresman.

Winterbottom, M. R. (1958). The relation of need for achievement to learning experiences in independence and mastery. In J. W. Atkinson (Ed.), *Motives in fantasy, action, and society.* Princeton, NJ: Van Nostrand.

Wolk, R. I., & Wolk, R. B. (1971). *Manual: Gerontological Apperception Test.* New York: Human Science Press.

Worchel, F. F., & Dupree, J. L. (1990). Projective storytelling techniques. In C. R. Reynolds & R. W. Kamphaus (Eds.), *Handbook of psychological and educational assessment of children: Personality, behavior, and context* (pp. 70–88). New York: Guilford.

Zubin, J. (1949). Personality research and psychopathology as related to clinical practice. *Journal of Abnormal and Social Psychology, 44,* 14–21.

Zubin, J., Eron, L. D., & Schumer, F. (1965). *An experimental approach to projective techniques.* New York: Wiley.

INDEX